Debate on
DISARMAMENT

Edited by
Michael Clarke and Marjorie Mowlam

Contributors
E. P. Thompson
Professor Johan Galtung
Reverend John Robinson
Mary Kaldor
Jonathan Dimbleby
Professor Michael Pentz

Routledge & Kegan Paul
London, Boston, Melbourne and Henley

First published in 1982
by Routledge & Kegan Paul Ltd
39 Store Street, London WC1E 7DD,
9 Park Street, Boston, Mass. 02108, USA,
296 Beaconsfield Parade, Middle Park,
Melbourne, 3206, Australia, and
Broadway House, Newtown Road,
Henley-on-Thames, Oxon RG9 1EN
Set in Bembo by
Input Typesetting Ltd, London
and printed in Great Britain by
T. J. Press (Padstow) Ltd
Padstow, Cornwall

ISBN 0–7100–9269–5

Contents

Acknowledgments

This book presents the lectures delivered under the title
'Perspectives on Disarmament' at the University of Newcastle
upon Tyne and sponsored by the Newcastle University Nuclear
Disarmament Group. The editors are grateful to a number of
people who have helped in compiling this book. Thanks are due
to Mike Adey, Jane Brooks, Celia Cornwell, Shelagh Groves,
Gail Langley, Heather Stewart, and Bryan Vernon for various
forms of help with transcripts of these lectures and drafts of the
final versions. Thanks are also due to everyone who helped in
staging the lecture series, and in particular to Dr A. L. Brown
both for his organisational ability and his help in writing some of
the editorial pieces for this volume. We would also like to thank
our contributors for all their co-operation, and their willingness
to respond so quickly to our deadlines.

Abridged versions of these six lectures appeared weekly in *New
Society* in November and December of 1981. Thanks are due to
that magazine's editor, Paul Barker, for all his help, and his
permission to use E. P. Thompson's article which was published
in *New Society*, 24 December 1981. Proceeds from the sale of this
book will go to the Newcastle University Nuclear Disarmament
Group.

Contributors

MARY KALDOR worked at the Stockholm International Peace Research Institute after reading PPE at Oxford. She has been a visiting fellow at MIT and in Berlin and now works in the Science Policy Research Unit in the University of Sussex. She has established herself as a leading critic and analyst of defence policy and international affairs.

JOHAN GALTUNG taught in Columbia University, New York, after graduating in Mathematics and Sociology in Norway. He has been Director of the International Peace Research Institute in Oslo and now works in the University Institute for the Study of Development in Geneva. He is a member of the Norwegian Academy of Sciences and Letters.

MICHAEL PENTZ was born in South Africa. He did physics research at the CERN Institute in Geneva until moving to the Open University, where he is Dean of Science, in 1969. He has become a leading figure in the disarmament movement and is a founder and chairman of Scientists Against Nuclear Arms.

THE RIGHT REVEREND JOHN ROBINSON has had an eminent career both as ecclesiastic and writer. When he was Bishop of Woolwich he published his best-known work *Honest to God*. He continues to publish regularly and gives lecture tours round the world. He is now Dean of Trinity College, Cambridge.

JONATHAN DIMBLEBY has worked for television since leaving university and is both a broadcaster and a journalist. He has published two books, contributes regularly to the *New Statesman* and produced the Yorkshire TV documentary *The Bomb* in 1980.

E. P. THOMPSON read history at Cambridge, lectured at the University of Leeds and held a Chair of History at the University of Warwick. He is well-known for his political and historical writing, especially for *The Making of the English Working Class*. He now writes full time and is one of the most active campaigners for European Nuclear Disarmament.

Introduction

The debate on disarmament is at once immediate, vociferous, controversial and has come upon us all surprisingly quickly. It is also a debate which is taking place at many different levels. It can therefore be most clearly understood when set in some kind of context. In this chapter we will examine the international background to the present interest in disarmament, the growth of the Peace Movement over the last two years, and finally, the British Government's response to both of these. In this way it is not difficult to understand why the issue of disarmament is so prevalent, or to appreciate why the immediate questions, values and underlying assumptions of disarmament have not been given the benefit of academic debate.

International background

There are some very obvious and immediate reasons why disarmament should have become such a live issue since 1979. The process of détente had been disappointing since 1975. Superpower relations became acrimonious again over Southern Africa, Iran, the 'Helsinki process' on European security, and particularly over arms control.[1] The Strategic Arms Limitation Talks (SALT) and, to a lesser extent, the Mutual and Balanced Force Reduction Talks have been the centrepiece of détente since 1969. Both have proved disappointing, and the failure of the United States to ratify the SALT II Treaty, signed in 1979 – a treaty which was extremely modest in relation to the problem of arms competition – has dealt a severe blow to the hopes of those who put faith in a gradualist approach to arms control.

In the light of this general development a series of govornmental and NATO decisions of the last three years attracted quite unexpected public attention. The British Government had to begin to make decisions about replacing Polaris submarines if Britain chose to remain an independent nuclear power. At the same time theatre nuclear forces, for use only within a European 'theatre' of war, became a public issue, particularly in the light of the US decision to deploy, and then to develop but not actually deploy, the neutron warhead. The concept of a limited nuclear war in Europe, and the whole notion of low-level nuclear forces being used as part of NATO's 'flexible response' to any attack, had always been problematical. Now the problems were being raised in public. So when NATO's ministers announced, in December 1979, a programme to modernise the West's theatre nuclear forces (TNFs) by introducing new systems, the public debate centred itself on the implications of this move.[2] The NATO ministers' decision was to introduce 572 cruise and Pershing II missiles as replacements for ageing bombers and older Pershing I missiles in response, they said, to Soviet modernisation programmes – particularly the introduction of the impressive SS-20 to replace the Soviets' obsolete SS-4s and SS-5s. At the same time NATO ministers declared their willingness to negotiate arms control agreements with the Soviets over these systems, the sanction being their eventual introduction should negotiations fail.

The deployment of the 572 missiles was to be spread among the allies: Italy, the Federal Republic of Germany, Belgium, the Netherlands and Britain. The NATO ministers' communiqué sounded definite and clear, but it disguised a fragile consensus: the Norwegian and Danish Governments were reportedly unconvinced by the seriousness of NATO's declared willingness to negotiate; the Italian and British Governments agreed to the deployment; the Federal Republic agreed, on condition that one further government did so; and Belgium and the Netherlands have effectively withheld their agreement to deploy the missiles until 1982.[3] The issue will reach a head in early 1982 as the West German Social Democrats vote at their Congress in April on whether or not to support the NATO decision. Actual deployment is due to begin in 1984. A well-known

American State Department official has declared that the whole issue is now 'the battle for the Soul of Europe'.[4]

Added to this there has emerged a public crisis of confidence in superpower management of European affairs, and of US leadership of the Atlantic Alliance in particular. The uncertainty of the Carter Administration, its public vacillation over the introduction of the neutron warhead (a hiatus that left the Federal Republic of Germany – its chief European ally – right out on a limb), the contradictory statements of senior officials in the Reagan Administration, and the emergence of so many near accidents in the deterrent systems operated by the US and NATO, have all contributed to a high level of public concern about nuclear weapons and have put the governments of the West on the defensive.[5] The behaviour of the Soviet Union in relation to Eastern Europe, in particular towards Poland, provokes different types of fear in the West, but it hardly inspires confidence.

This accumulation of controversial issues has not, however, occurred by accident. It is possible to see them in a longer term perspective, as symptoms of deeper trends that have received far less public attention. Relations within the Atlantic Alliance have been strained for some time. Even in the heyday of détente, from the mid-1960s to the mid-1970s, as the terms of the Cold War seemed to be changing, the emergence of significant differences of interest among the Western allies threatened the consensus within NATO. There was inadequate consultation, increasing economic competition both inside and outside NATO, and persistent European worries that their individual strategic and political interests were being compromised by the superpower dialogue. And since détente has gone sour in the last seven years these differences have become even more acute as more contentious international issues have arisen: Southern Africa, the Arab-Israeli conflict and the implications for energy supplies, American hostages in Iran, reactions to the Afghanistan crisis and the Olympic boycott, and in 1981–2, the Polish crisis. No amount of fence mending, 'new Atlantic Charters', 'Years of Europe' or 'new beginnings' as introduced by successive US Administrations have been able to halt a general split in Atlantic relations.[6]

Strategic issues have therefore become particularly significant. Some European governments do not see the 'Soviet
threat' in anything like the same terms as the United States;
the Reagan Administration is exasperated that European
governments do not do more to mobilise their publics to
recognise the threat. Meanwhile European governments
have difficulty reconciling contradictory and unguarded
American statements about nuclear weapons policy to their
increasingly sceptical constituents.

The late 1970s has also been a time when, for technological
reasons, NATO has had to face its first set of major and
conspicuous decisions for almost twenty years on the real
implications of its strategy. For the doctrine of 'flexible response' was adopted by NATO governments after much
quiet agonising in 1966.[7] By this time, the nuclear weapons
that would be involved in this strategy were already deployed. Pershing I missiles and the Soviets' SS-4s and SS-5s,
the nuclear artillery of both sides, and some of the aircraft,
were introduced into Europe in the late 1950s and early
1960s.[8] The allies, did not, therefore, have to take any major
weapons decisions in order to implement the doctrine of
flexible response. It remained ambiguous and relatively un-
contentious, as all deterrent threats should remain ambiguous, since to spell them out clearly can render them either
incredible or ineffective. With the continuing competition in
armaments, however, the late 1970s have presented both
sides with the problem of modernising their TNFs. NATO
governments now have to take a series of important decisions
– on neutron warheads, cruise and Pershing II missiles, new
aircraft – in order, they believe, to continue to implement a
deterrent strategy of flexible response. But the new weapons
are so advanced by comparison with the old, that they may,
in themselves, destabilise the whole deterrent system in Europe. Decisions forced upon NATO governments by the
imperatives of technology have opened up debate about the
real implications of a nuclear, flexible response, while at the
same time calling into question the very stability such
weapons are supposed to maintain.

Finally, the present European concern over disarmament
is also part of a more general world-wide interest in the

problem, expressed through the publicity given to the United Nations Special Sessions on Disarmament, and the work of the permanent disarmament committee in Geneva.[9] Third World states have become more vociferous in their criticisms of the East-West arms race, in particular because of the encouragement a 'central' arms race may give to nuclear proliferation in other geographical areas, but also because of the effects such an arms race is believed to have in starving the process of development of finance, technical initiative and higher political priorities. The Brandt Report clearly made such a connection.[10] There is, in other words, a more favourable international climate in which to consider the possibilities of and necessity for disarmament. The disorder in world economic relations and the growing regional threats to peace, throw into stark relief an apparently endless and increasingly costly East-West arms race which the philosophy of arms control (which had effectively displaced constructive thinking about disarmament since the early 1950s) has done little to modify.

The growth of the Peace Movement

What has come to be known as the Peace Movement has quickly grown in the last few years throughout Europe. In Britain, using membership of the Campaign for Nuclear Disarmament (CND) as an indicator, a sharp increase in support can be registered from late 1979 continuing through 1980–1. This upturn in membership parallels the election of a new and strident British Government in 1979 and the decision in March 1980 to site 160 cruise missiles in Oxfordshire and East Anglia. Monsignor Bruce Kent shows that membership also increased after November 1979 when US aircraft and missile bases were put on a six minute alert after a computer test tape had been transmitted by mistake.[11] In 1979 CND public donations doubled and for the first time since 1960 the number of staff employed by CND was increased.[12]

The clear escalation in support for CND in the 1980s can be seen as having its roots in the years 1975–80. Since 1975 the film *The War Game* which the BBC had officially banned since 1965 had been watched by an estimated quarter of a million people. 1976 saw a steep rise in the sale of CND publications and a noticeable increase in attendance at CND organised public meetings. In 1977, the Scottish branch of CND transported more than 1,000 demonstrators by paddle steamer to the US base at Holy Loch. During 1978 CND collected over 250,000 signatures to a petition against the neutron bomb and campaigned vigorously in support of the declaration of the United Nations Special Session on Disarmament of that year.[13]

By the end of 1980 CND membership had risen from an estimated 4,000 to over 9,000. Hundreds of new groups had been formed including viable Irish and Welsh branches. The election of President Reagan in November 1980 with his emphasis on defence spending, together with the Conservative Government's increase in defence spending, gave CND a further boost in membership.[14] The CND annual conference of 1980 in Leeds was attended by over 300 delegates. Moves to make CND into a political party failed. Resolutions were framed looking to broaden the base of support for the organisation: although conference did accept a resolution that union members should be encouraged to oppose production and movement of nuclear weapons.

By the time of its annual conference in 1981, CND membership had increased to about 300,000 members. The strength of its membership made accusations of it being a puppet of left-wing manipulators impossible to sustain. As Monsignor Bruce Kent, general secretary of CND, said at the conference: 'Dr Luns of NATO has lied in his claim that Western peace movements have received massive funding from the Soviet Union; but mud sticks.'[15] CND's continuing desire to avoid close identification with a single party is illustrated by the reversal of the conference decision of the previous year so that from 1981 onwards unions and the Labour movement were not the primary campaigning target, and CND decided not to adopt 'Jobs not Bombs' as its official slogan. At the same time Joan Ruddock, a Labour Party prospective candidate, was elected chairperson of CND.

The objective of CND today is, as it has always been, the unilateral renunciation by Britain of nuclear weapons. As always its main source of finance is from membership subscriptions; these being sufficient that by the end of 1981 CND employed ten full-time and two short-term workers.

The British Peace Movement in 1980 and 1981 has not only grown in terms of the size of CND. A Marplan poll indicated that more people favoured unilateral nuclear disarmament in 1980 than had done at the height of the campaign in the 1960s. Of the British people 41 per cent favoured a ban on all nuclear weapons on British soil.[16] Specific support for the Peace Movement came most notably from political parties, trade unions, churches and professional groups such as scientists and writers. We will examine briefly the growth of support from each organisation in turn and then compare the growth of the British Peace Movement with that in Europe.

The Peace Movement in Britain has the support of three of the political parties: Labour, Ecology and Liberal. Before the 1980 Liberal Party Assembly the Liberal National Council had passed a motion opposing cruise missiles, a decision that had led to conflict in the parliamentary Liberal Party. This decision was partially reversed at the Liberal Party Assembly in 1981 when by 533 to 455 votes a motion calling for a non-nuclear defence strategy was rejected. By September 1981 delegates at the Liberal Party Assembly condemned the production of neutron warheads and opposed the basing of cruise missiles in Europe with a resolution that was unilateralist in nature. The pacifist president of the Liberal Party, Viv Bingham, acknowledges the differences between the Liberal Party's unilateral policy and the multilateral policy of their alliance partners, the SDP. He argues that 'it simply means we have a bigger parish to convert.'[17] He quotes as a positive sign of early co-operation a backbenchers' motion in the House of Commons calling for a comprehensive test ban treaty. It urges that the United Nations Special Session on Disarmament in June 1982 should give priority to the treaty. Other Liberals are concerned that the Liberals in the alliance will work for peace by words alone and that unilateral principles will be sold out for the advantages of the political power that the alliance will possibly bring.

The Labour Party at its national conference in 1980 re-affirmed the support it gave in 1972 for unilateral nuclear disarmament. 143 resolutions and 19 amendments were presented to this conference on nuclear weapons. In addition the Labour Party gave its official backing to the CND demonstration planned for October 1980 as well as organising its first ever demonstration for peace in June 1980 (a demonstration the police said was attended by 15,000 people, while the Labour Party organisers put the figures as high as 20,000–30,000 people).[18] Support for unilateral policies was far from unanimous. Many multilateralists in the party, like David Owen and Dennis Healey, were far from happy and ex-party leader, James Callaghan, dissociated himself from the party's official support for the CND rally. The 1981 Labour Party conference had ninety-two resolutions on disarmament – more than on any other subject. Conference passed a motion for an 'unambiguous commitment to unilateral disarmament' by 4,596,000 votes to 2,315,000. This defence motion also declared unconditional opposition to the deployment of cruise missiles and all other nuclear weapons in Britain. A motion calling for an immediate withdrawal from NATO was soundly defeated. Much debate has ensued in the Labour Party since these conference decisions. Mainly because the vote on unilateralism did not receive a two-thirds majority it does not by perforce become party policy, as Brynmor John and others opposed to unilateralism do not hesitate to point out.

At a local level, across the political party spectrum, local nuclear-free zones had been declared by 120 councils by the end of 1981. With local differences and variations these councils have rejected nuclear weapons, the transport of nuclear materials and the value of a civil defence programme as a viable form of protection in a nuclear war. South Yorkshire was the first council to declare itself a nuclear-free zone in September 1980, quickly followed by Manchester who set about writing to all other councils urging them to follow suit. The Association of Metropolitan Authorities, which represents city and metropolitan county councils in England, has given endorsement to these councils. Many, like the Greater London Council, are taking steps to translate such declarations into practical policies, as for example the Greater London Council's recent creation of a research group to examine the links between disarmament and jobs.

Support for nuclear disarmament has increased among trade unions to such an extent in the last two years that at its annual conference in September 1981, the TUC adopted a resolution that unequivocally supported unilateral nuclear disarmament; the first time that the TUC has ever taken such a stance.[19] The motion put forward by the transport workers, train drivers and bakers suggested that the most important issue facing the world today is safeguarding peace and détente. It opposed the Tory Government's policy of increasing its reliance on a defence policy based on nuclear weapons and called on the Labour Party to include a policy declaration in its next election manifesto based on reducing arms expenditure and the closure of all nuclear bases in Britain.

Progress in individual unions is even more dramatic. ASTMS affiliated to CND in 1980 by executive decision. At their conference in 1981 they carried a motion congratulating the National Executive Committee of the Labour Party on the party's unilateral motion, thus affirming the union's support for unilateral disarmament. The ASTMS conference also called for a campaign for the withdrawal of Britain from NATO. In 1980 the APEX annual conference had one motion opposing nuclear weapons; by 1981 it had eleven. Similarly the Transport and General Workers had five motions on nuclear weapons in 1980, but this jumped to thirty in the space of one year.

Even more striking were the eleven motions on the 1981 conference agenda of the Society of Civil and Public Servants – the union which organises executive and directing grades in the Civil Service, Civil Service unions at first appeared positive in their support for CND, but this had not materialised during 1981. The biggest Civil Service union has backtracked on a conference decision to affiliate to CND – to allay protests from its influential Ministry of Defence membership. The decision at the annual conference of the Civil and Public Service Association in May 1980 to affiliate to CND is now under review.[20]

NUPE, the public employees union has been affiliated to CND for many years. At its conference in 1981 it called for the removal of all nuclear bases from Britain. The motion was carried with only four votes against. APEX and US-DAW have both debated motions on nuclear disarmament in 1981. Motions on disarmament have appeared on the APEX conference agenda for some years, but not until last year had the subject been given a sufficiently high priority to have time allocated to it for debate. Both unions carried motions in support of disarmament: a multilateral one from APEX and a unilateral one from USDAW. At their 1981 annual conference in Bournemouth NATFHE voted to press for an element of peace education to be included in teacher training syllabuses and in-service programmes. It is the first time that this 73,000-strong union has passed a policy on disarmament.[21]

The Peace Movement is therefore making inroads into the unions. However from the information listed above it would be wrong to assume that a majority of union members themselves have rejected the case for nuclear weapons. There is, as many nuclear disarmers within the union movement admit, a long way to go in educating and informing union members of the nuclear debate. This is particularly true of unions such as the biggest engineering union, the AUEW, which sees nuclear disarmament as a threat to jobs. A similar problem is acknowledged in the GMWU. Although discussion has taken place on steps towards unilateralism, there is still a great deal of ambivalence on the issue. As James Morrell, the Scottish regional secretary of the union stated, more than one-tenth of the membership are employed in industries related to defence spending and so 'for that reason we have not been in favour of freezing or cutting defence spending.'[22]

There is no doubt that the base of support for the Peace Movement is increasing. By the end of 1980 evidence of support had come from doctors in the Medical Association for the Prevention of War and also from such diverse groups as lawyers, artists and musicians. In March 1981 the inaugural conference of Scientists Against Nuclear Arms (SANA) took place. The main role of this new organisation is to provide reliable and accurate information to peace and disarmament organisations, and to groups and individuals with influence over public policy. Later in the year a group of doctors from Europe, the United States and the Soviet Union (including the personal physician of Brezhnev) banded together to fight what they see as the world's most dangerous health hazard – nuclear war. This was widely publicised in the United States and the Soviet Union, but little notice was taken of it in Britain. The group, calling themselves the International Physicians for the Prevention of Nuclear War, concluded their first meeting with the statement that any organised medical response to nuclear war could 'make no significant difference to its catastrophic effects.'[23]

Artists and musicians have for a long time been active supporters of nuclear disarmament. 'Poets Against the Bomb' made a film including such performers as Brian Patten, Adrian Mitchell, Harold Pinter and others. In August 1981, 150 European writers including twenty-three East Germans signed an appeal for an end to the arms race. The document claims that: 'Humanity is to be made used to the criminal idea that it is possible to conduct a limited nuclear war with new rockets, neutron bombs, cruise missiles, etc.' The appeal started by the Association of German Writers and signed by such eminent writers as Heinrich Böll and Günter Grass is supported by authors' associations in Finland, the Netherlands, France, Italy and Yugoslavia. The importance of such groups lies not in their numbers; there have always been such organisations which come and go at various times. But their existence indicates the breadth of support for disarmament and their various conclusions are surprisingly unanimous.

The churches, particularly the Methodist Church and the British Council of Churches, have taken a growing interest in disarmament. The British Council of Churches gave its blessing to the formation of the World Disarmament Campaign. Much discussion has taken place in the churches in the last two years as to how they can best support the resurgent CND. At the CND rally in 1980 there was an absence of Christian organisations, except for the Quakers and the Roman Catholic Pax Christi Movement.[74] The churches have been encouraged to respond to the growing Peace Movement by the rapid and marked interest in readers' letters both unsolicited and responding to the leading articles on the topic of nuclear weapons in religious journals. The *Methodist Recorder* notes how unusual it is for one particular issue to stimulate such an amazing response. *The Times* comments 'it is difficult to give the phenomenon any other interpretation than that it marks a groundswell of public uneasiness with the standard defence of nuclear deterrence policy and an inclination to move towards a unilateralist position.'[25]

No governing assembly of any national church has as yet adopted a unilateralist stance, although some seem to be edging their way there. The pressure is invariably being felt from below – a reversal of the usual process of leadership. The Methodists and the Roman Catholics have embarked on an official review of the arguments. As yet only the Quakers and the Roman Catholics have an official agency with the word 'peace' in the title. The General Synod of the Church of England has not yet responded but with pressure from individual members and a request in the *Methodist Recorder* that the British Council of Churches set up a peace committee, the Church of England cannot continue to ignore the situation. The churches have responded in a wide variety of ways to the issue of nuclear disarmament: from a peace pilgrimage across the Alps, to a bishop urging workers on the neutron bomb to quit their jobs; from a 900-mile bicycle peace pilgrimage to Canterbury, to the organisation of a religious summit for peace being planned for the autumn of 1982. Church leaders of many denominations feel that the disarmament issue is one on which the churches should take a lead.[26] As Cardinal Hume said in a letter to the British Government; it should disarm and restore the cuts in overseas aid to help the world's poor. Similarly, forty Baptist leaders from ten countries who met in Moscow in June 1981 called on governments to cease new arms developments and further weapon installations in Europe.[27]

One religious leader who has taken a clear stance is the

secretary of the Methodist conference, Kenneth Greer. He has put enormous energy into the formation of the World Disarmament Campaign (WDC). WDC is an umbrella organisation for a wide variety of groups – pacifist, humanitarian and religious – which are united in the desire to pressure organisations such as the United Nations to work positively towards peace. The impetus behind the creation of the WDC is the belief that the multilateral versus unilateral divisions in the Peace Movement are oversimplified. Supporters of WDC hold to the view that all forms of nuclear protest are good in as much as they create such a clamour as to force the governments of the world to adopt real disarmament policies. Such a clamour, such a degree of public bother, means that the non-disarmament option becomes closed, and the problem for governments then becomes how to make the best of the remaining possibilities.

WDC is staffed (at the end of 1981) by five full-time and two part-time workers. Its running costs average about £1,200 a week. It is supported primarily by the Methodist Church but also the British Council of Churches, Oxfam, Christian Aid, War on Want and a leading charitable trust. Oxfam gave very generously at the initiation of WDC. The first secretary of the WDC, Brigadier Michael Harbottle, former chief of staff of the UN peacekeeping force in Cyprus, claims that by October 1981 there were 450 groups representing between 80,000 and 100,000 people in Britain.[28]

At the first meeting in April 1980 of the WDC at Central Hall, Westminster, attended by over 2,000 people, Cardinal Hume emphasised the importance of the *world* aspect of the WDC. He said care must be taken not to turn the Soviet Union into the 'bogeyman'. It is possible, he argued, to drift into a war no one wanted 'simply on the assumption that we are faced with a sinister adversary.'[29] The WDC has launched a world-wide petition which is being organised on a national basis, constituency by constituency, door to door. It is to be presented to the UN General Assembly Special Session in 1982. Its basic demands are:

1 the abolition of nuclear weapons and all weapons of mass destruction;
2 the abolition by agreed stages of conventional arms, leading to,
3 general and complete disarmament;
4 transference of military expenditure to end world poverty.

The Japanese already have 25 million signatures on this petition.

The WDC has not been the only attempt to broaden the base of support for the Peace Movement. The many and diverse disarmament activities throughout Europe were finding it difficult to achieve a coordinated impact. European Nuclear Disarmament (END) was created in order to remedy this. END was launched at the same time as WDC in April 1980. The objectives of END are the same as CND – only more so. They are to promote the removal of nuclear weapons from the whole of Europe, East and West, by any means that may present themselves as effective: unilateral, multilateral, etc. Its main aim is to disseminate information both by pamphlets and public meetings and to work to coordinate the Peace Movement in Europe. It has two full-time workers and raises most of its money by fund-raising appeals. In the last year most of the money was collected by a fund-raising speaking tour of the United States by END's leading light, E. P. Thompson. END does not have individual members because it works closely with CND and does not want to compete for membership subscriptions.

The extent of a European-wide nuclear disarmament movement can best be illustrated by the figures in Table 1 which show the support for mass demonstrations throughout Europe by December 1981.[30] Given the geographical extent of Europe and the cost of travelling it is unlikely that US Defense Secretary Weinberger's allegation is valid that the Peace Movement is made up of the same people forever milling around Europe 'like marbles on a tray'. So how do the individual European Peace Movements differ?

There is a clear distinction between the north and the south. The major section of interest can be found in the northern 'Nordic' areas – Norway, Sweden, Denmark and

Table 1 Support for nuclear disarmament demonstrations in Europe, October to December 1981

Date	Place	Numbers attending demonstration	Compared to total population of country (in millions)
24 October	Bonn	300,000	61.3 (FRG)
24 October	Helsinki	80,000	4.5 (Finland)
24 October	Oslo	10,000	4.0 (Norway)
24 October	London	250,000	55.0 (UK)
24 October	Rome	500,000	60.1 (Italy)
25 October	Brussels	250,000	9.0 (Belgium)
25 October	Paris	50,000	50.0 (France)
25 October	Potsdam	50,000	16.7 (GDR)
15 November	Madrid	500,000	30.0 (Spain)
21 November	Amsterdam	500,000	11.5 (Netherlands)
6 December	Athens	500,000	9.0 (Greece)

Finland – where there are no nuclear weapons. The movement is probably strongest in Norway where a Norwegian opinion poll in August 1981 showed that 53 per cent of the population were in favour of a nuclear-free zone in the north. This groundswell of support has suffered the recent setback of a newly elected government which is opposed to a Nordic nuclear-free zone. The Norwegian Peace Movement is rather similar to the one in Britain being non-aligned, well-informed, and a tightly organised movement lobbying extensively for support at every level. It has some trade union support and a good deal of church support. In a curious sort of way the Norwegian movement has a clear lineage back to the Norwegian resistance movement.

In Holland there are two movements at work: the first a popular street-based campaigning organisation with some Communist influence called *Stop de Neutronen bom*; and the second the more influential Dutch Inter-Peace Council – this being the most experienced non-aligned campaigning group in Europe. The council has coined the slogan 'Ban nuclear

weapons from the world, starting with the Netherlands.'
The church in Holland has had a strong impact, arguing as
it does that the Western alliance has to lead the way in
disarmament in the hope that the Warsaw Pact will follow.
Holland also has an important group in the *Vredesen Veiligh-*
eidsberaad Kriggsmacht, VVBK (Peace and Security Discussion
Group in the Armed Forces) which is a small group opposed
to nuclear weapons. Its existence worries the Dutch Ministry
of Defence as the results of a preliminary survey in 1979
showed that half of the army is opposed to the use of nuclear
weapons.[31]

The disarmament movement in Germany is of more recent
origins and is better understood in terms of a multitude of
movements rather than a single one. There is the Action
Reconciliation, the German Protestant Church Movement,
the dissident or critical wing of the SDP, the Green Party,
the Ecology Party and the various left wing groups. In August 1981 60,000 Germans attended a rally near the Reichstag
protesting against President Reagan's decision to introduce
the neutron bomb.[32] However, a poll by the Allensbach
Institute earlier in the same month showed that West German
public opinion was certainly not drifting quickly into neu-
tralism: 78 per cent of those questioned wanted to stay in
NATO.

The movement in France is the most sluggish of all the
European countries as, like the UK, France has its own
nuclear weapons not to mention a Socialist Government
which supports their existence.[33]

In the south of Europe the movement is more limited
within societies where party politics tend be all pervasive. In
Italy for example a mass following for disarmament only
really blossomed in the latter half of 1981, consisting of the
Radical Party and more recently the Italian Eurocommunist
Party. In Spain campaigners are directing their energies to
keeping their country out of NATO. In Ireland CND is
campaigning hard to keep Ireland neutral and resist further
NATO activity on the west coast.

The coming to power in Greece of the Socialist PASOK
Party is a positive step for the disarmament movement as
Papandreou committed himself before the election to initiate

a nuclear-free zone in the Balkans within the first six months of coming to power. Under the NATO 'double key system' Greece has stockpiles of artillery, surface-to-surface and surface-to-air weapons. It is not clear if the removal of these would be a unilateral act or conditional on the other Balkan states accepting this plan.[34]

The future of END depends on the crucial tests of the next year; that is, can the Peace Movement in West Europe establish solid links with Central and East Europe; can the disarmament movement, in the words of E. P. Thompson, 'go behind the missiles to the Cold War itself?' These links and exchanges are starting, but very slowly. There are official links between the Peace Movement and peace committees and other government bodies in Central and East Europe. Reuter reports that the Rumanian leader Nicolai Ceaucescu called in October 1981 for the removal of Soviet weapons from Europe and for NATO to revoke nuclear modernisation plans. Thompson and other END activists think that, particularly after Poland, direct contact with governments is necessary, but this is not the most fruitful avenue of activity. A more important level of activity is the quasi official level where specialist groups, professionals and citizens can contact each other across the East-West divide. This is already happening with groups in the churches, universities, trade unions and writers. This is the activity which must continue if the Peace Movement is to have a successful future.

The Government response

The British Government has had to face the Peace Movement at an awkward time for British defence policy: it is under pressure from the United States and other NATO allies to maintain the commitment undertaken at Venice in May 1977 to increase defence expenditure by 3 per cent in real terms per year; it is looking for cuts in public expenditure all round and 'military' inflation is higher than 'domestic' inflation; in July 1980 it announced its decision to buy the Trident missile system from the United States to replace Polaris, but is unsure what the eventual cost will be (£6,000 million is the bottom official estimate); and it has agreed to accept cruise and Pershing II missiles at a time when large sections of both public and official opinion in Europe seem to be turning against their deployment. British defence policy in 1980 and 1981 has, in short, been under financial and political siege. It is at the centre not only of a public debate on disarmament and an alternative defence policy, but also of an official reassessment of costs, roles, and feasibilities.[35] Britain's role in the nuclear balance has therefore been subject to more official debate in 1980–1 than at any time since Britain became a nuclear power.

In January 1981 Mr John Nott was appointed Minister of Defence and gave fresh impetus to cost-cutting in British defence policy. There followed five months of well-publicised blood-letting in the Ministry of Defence (MoD) as it became clear, despite official denials, that the costs of Trident would affect spending in other areas of defence.[36] The annual Defence White Paper was published in April and debated in parliament in May. It attempted to rationalise the cost-cutting exercise and made it clear that the navy had lost this particular internal battle and the surface fleet would have to be reduced. Mr Keith Speed, Under Secretary of State for the Navy, denounced the shift in resources and was sacked. Mr Speed had been involved in detailed work on Trident. His rebellion was an indication of how difficult the problem of paying for the new deterrent had become for the three services. In June Mr Nott's own defence reappraisal appeared, entitled *The Way Forward*. It was the sixth major review of defence policy since 1945, trying to reassess priorities. It made clear that no area of defence was beyond scrutiny, but, equally, that the commitment to Trident was absolute though costs were still uncertain. No sooner was *The Way Forward* debated, however, than its provisions were being modified by further infighting in the Ministry of Defence and heavy pressure from the Treasury for its spending projections to be revised.[37] Parliament's own Select Committee on Defence had failed to agree on the costs and necessity for Trident. As John Nott's review was being debated, the Select Committee published a majority (Conservative)

and minority (Labour) report on the new missile which re-
hearsed all the arguments and failed to arrive at any clear
conclusion.[38] The Government was known to be worried
about the Select Committee's minority report and tried to
play down publicity for it by concentrating on the debate
surrounding *The Way Forward*. In October it became clear
that the United States would opt for the more expensive
Trident II missile, and that as a result Britain would almost
certainly have to do the same at an additional cost of around
£1,000 million. Mr Nott admitted that this was indeed the
case.[39] Apart from the Government's determination to have
it, little had become clear about the Trident project by the
end of 1981. In a Commons debate in November, Mr Nott
was still unwilling to announce just what form the Trident
force would take, or what it might cost, but repeated an
assurance – already belied by the 1981 Defence White Paper
and his own review – that 'there is no reason for conventional
forces to be adversely affected.'[40]

On top of this, the Government has had to react to the
political disarray within NATO, the growing opposition to
the whole principle behind the Trident decision, and the
problems posed by statements from the US Administration.
President Reagan's decision in August 1981 to proceed with
the development of the neutron warhead was a good example. European allies were dismayed at the lack of consultation preceding this announcement (given the problems the
warhead had caused them in 1978). The British Government
had to maintain that this was an internal matter for the
United States, but still could not disguise the fact that such
an announcement played into the hands of the Peace Movement. The Government is facing, therefore, not only the
economic dilemmas of deterrence as the cost of new technology has to be borne, but also the political and democratic
dilemmas, as the implications of political control of new
technology becomes more conspicuously problematic.

In the light of these circumstances the response of the
Government to the growth of the disarmament lobby has
been interesting. There have been no shifts in substantive
policy. It would be strange if there had been since the present
Conservative Party, whether in or out of office, has always

been strongly committed to a defence policy involving nuclear forces. It is also very unlikely to change its policy in response to a lobby which is still in a minority in the country, no matter how convincing or articulate the arguments of that lobby may be. Nevertheless, if a Marplan public opinion poll published in April 1981 is correct, the disarmament lobby is becoming a substantial minority and has attracted unexpected levels of support on specific disarmament issues, particularly on their opposition to Trident missiles.[41] It shows every sign of being a relevant minority in electoral terms. What has shifted is the presentation of the Government's policy. Ministers are now far more assertive in their pronouncements on nuclear issues and have made a point of answering Peace Movement arguments in speeches and statements.

The number of local councils that, by late 1980, had publicly declared their opposition to co-operating with the Government's civil defence plans appears to have triggered a reaction in Whitehall and a resolve to explain its defence policy more openly. The 1981 Defence White Paper was unique in that it contained a section headed 'Nuclear weapons and preventing war', which Mr Nott referred to as a 'nuclear essay.'[42] This was, in fact, written by Mr Michael Quinlan of the MoD and set out, for the first time in such documents, a rationale for Britain's deterrent policy. At the same time the MoD, and to a lesser extent the Foreign Office (FCO), began to issue more direct fact sheets and briefing papers to convey the deterrent argument more forcefully to the public. Mr Nott openly admitted that the Government were to engage in an active public relations campaign to wean 'innocent, well-meaning people' away from the superficially attractive ideas of CND – a campaign which was heavily influenced by a tiny number of left-wingers who were 'neither innocent nor well-meaning'. The Soviets, he said, would exploit any successful peace campaign in the West.[43]

As the Peace Movement's programme of activities attracted such publicity in the autumn of 1981, there was a barrage of official speeches in reaction to them. Mr Nott vigorously attacked the TUC's support for unilateralism as being 'totally out of line with the feelings of the people'.[44]

He even went out of his way to comment in response to CND's 1981 Annual Conference, referring to unilateralism here as a 'cul-de-sac.'[45] Meanwhile, the former Minister of Defence, Mr Francis Pym, warned that the West was in danger of losing popular support for totally justified defence policies because 'we are not explaining it enough.'[46] Mr Peter Blaker, Minister of State at the FCO, directly attacked the 'twelve fallacies' of the CND movement in a well-reported speech;[47] Mrs Thatcher spoke in several interviews and parliamentary questions of the dangers of the Peace Movement's approach, and Lord Carrington, the Foreign Secretary, weighed in with a major speech in Luxemburg on 27 October which heavily criticised the European Peace Movement, and British groups in particular, for engaging in a campaign that would have unintended and dangerous consequences.[48]

It was with some relief that Mr Nott welcomed the publication by the United States of *Soviet Military Power* in October 1981, which was the public version of a series of briefings previously given to European NATO ministers in the United States to impress upon them the nature of the Soviet threat.[49] And President Reagan's announcement of his 'zero option' proposal was 'unreservedly welcomed' by the Prime Minister.[50] For this could be presented as putting the ball firmly in the Soviet court and could take some of the steam out of the Peace Movement's demands.

The Government's policy on nuclear weapons is, in outline, very well known: to maintain an independent deterrent and follow the US lead in replacing Polaris with Trident submarine-launched missiles; to support NATO's TNF modernisation plans and agree to the introduction of cruise and Pershing II missiles; and to help revive the flagging consensus within the NATO alliance by supporting the deployment of new weapon systems, as much on psychological as military grounds, in order to maintain the sense of *political* commitment that is indispensable to making *military* deterrence credible.

The vigorous defence of these broad outlines, however, has served the purpose of making explicit four important assumptions which underlie the Government's policy that previously had only been implicit. First, there are a number of assumptions made about the basic idea of deterrence. Weapons of deterrence are *not* weapons intended for war-fighting. 'The idea', said Mr Nott in the Commons, 'that any Western democratic nation could conceive of Trident or any other nuclear weapon being required for war fighting is too fanciful for words.'[51] The argument that new technologies open up various possibilities of war fighting as well as war prevention, is not acknowledged officially to make any difference to the working of deterrence – certainly not in the case of Western nations. Deterrence is also explicitly assumed to have worked in keeping the peace of Europe since 1945. Most Government pronouncements have prefaced their remarks with this assertion. Lord Carrington probably expressed it most concisely when he said that it was an observation dictated by commonsense.[52] To challenge the working of deterrence, therefore, is to challenge the basis – indeed the structure – of peace in Europe. As the 1981 Defence White Paper says, 'to tear down the present structure, imperfect but effective, before a better one is firmly within our grasp would be an immensely dangerous and irresponsible act.'[53] And in being a structure, deterrence is not simply a military phenomenon. To be credible, it must be backed by the political willpower to use the military instrument. Therefore anything which threatens to compromise such political willpower can be seen as destabilising. Deterrence is thus a structure on these assumptions because it includes everything. So any rows which threaten the consensus within NATO, or any hesitancy in our resolve to deploy new weapons, may be seen, regardless of the technical or military arguments, to threaten the West's nuclear strategy. Mr Humphrey Atkins, FCO spokesman in the Commons, said in the foreign affairs debate in November: 'Once we appear to be weakening or flinching in our resolve to defend ourselves, then the temptation to threaten and blackmail will grow.'[54] Or, as Mr Nott told MPs, the calculation of effective deterrence 'comes down to judgment and commonsense'.[55] Deterrence is thus seen to be a political, more than a military device, to which there can be no gradual alternative. It must be maintained, and cannot be compromised, unless or until there is as complete an alternative structure to replace it.

A second set of assumptions are revealed concerning the relative priorities of nuclear risks in terms of other national interests: while *technologically* nuclear arms are seen to be qualitatively different from conventional weapons, in *political* terms they are not regarded as a new species of defence. National defence is necessary to preserve 'our freedom which we have defended against all-comers for so many centuries'.[56] Nuclear weapons are now the essence of our defence, so nuclear weapons are a guarantee of freedom. Mrs Thatcher argued very much along this line in a spontaneous answer to a parliamentary question on 24 July 1981, when she said that we would put our way of life at risk without a nuclear deterrent.[57] Or again, on the Jimmy Young radio programme she argued strongly for the development of the neutron bomb. It was necessary because: 'A bully goes for the weakest. If the Soviet Union ever threatened us we would be in a position to deliver a devastating blow.'[58] In other words, while under the first set of assumptions, deterrence works – indeed is inevitable – as a mechanism to prevent war, under these assumptions, war may not be the last resort. There are national interests above the risks of nuclear war; things to be preserved by the time-honoured resort to national defence. In this vein much has been made of the privilege disarmers enjoy to demonstrate, which would not be available were we to relinquish nuclear weapons and so be subject to Soviet domination. Just as the original decision to become a nuclear weapons power in the 1940s and the decision to improve the warheads of Polaris missiles in the 1970s were taken on the automatic assumption that a modern defence system simply required it, so recent decisions have similarly appeared to be inevitable. We need to be a nuclear power because the stronger we are, the more we are capable of defending ourselves.[59] Of course, defence as a means of preventing war, and defence as a means of preserving a way of life, are not incompatible. But the assumption that *nuclear* defence is designed to preserve national interests may not be compatible with the assumption that it is 'too fanciful for words' to regard it as a war-fighting instrument. In short, thinking about defence as a task to perform is not entirely consistent with thinking about deterrence as a dilemma to be resolved.

At the very least, these traditional assumptions about strength and defence make it difficult to conceive of a radical alternative type of defence policy. For the 'strength equals defence' argument will always gravitate towards more of the same in equipment and tactics. Thus, even now, it would take a long time and a huge political effort to alter a British defence policy based on modern strategic nuclear weapons, a heavily armoured Rhine Army, a 'forward-based' air force, nuclear artillery, and, perhaps, a new generation of offensive cruise and Pershing II missiles.[60]

Third, Government arguments also rest heavily on the assumption that there is a balance of political and military power in Europe, which can be calculated, and must be preserved. The Soviet deployment of SS-20 missiles has been repeatedly used as the justification for the need to modernise NATO's TNFs. The balance, it is said, is moving against the West. Cruise and Pershing II missiles will restore it, if negotiations do not. In parliament, Mrs Thatcher found it 'remarkable' that this logic was not obvious to a Labour questioner.[61] Apart from the fact that this apparently simple relationship between new missiles and SS-20s is not supported by the background to NATO's decision in 1979, it also reveals a number of facets of official thinking about this balance.[62] It assumes, for instance, that the Soviet Union is automatically a threat, so that any notable imbalance of military strength will inevitably be exploited. Evidence for this is drawn from Soviet behaviour in Africa, Afghanistan and Eastern Europe, with the necessary corollary that it would apply to Western Europe. It is also assumed that the Soviet Union and the Warsaw Pact have overwhelming conventional superiority in Europe, and this asymmetry in the balance is deliberately compensated by the West's superiority – and determination to remain superior – in deterrent weapons. Time after time, this juxtaposition is made. Michael Mates, Conservative MP for Petersfield, expressed it very clearly when he wrote that NATO's deterrent was 'perhaps the reason that the Russians have not swept through Northern Europe to the Channel ports with their superior conventional forces.'[63] Geoffrey Pattie, Under Secretary for Defence, stressed the same point in parliament, adding that, 'The cost of matching the East [in conventional weapons] would be huge, socially and culturally, to the point of political unacceptability.'[64] The threat is therefore automatic and obvious; it can be calculated, and is a function of the degree of overall military balance in Europe. This line of thinking is constantly strengthened by reference to appeasement in the 1930s, and the consequences of allowing an imbalance to tempt a natural aggressor.

Even if it is accepted that the motives for a Soviet invasion may be lacking, the line of argument is still influential, for a nuclear Soviet Union facing a non-nuclear Western Europe would, it is argued, then be in a position to 'blackmail' us, in which case, as Peter Blaker said, 'our conventional armaments would have the value of scrap metal.'[65] How such pressure might actually work is not made clear.

This need to maintain some sort of overall military balance, therefore, reveals a received wisdom (derived very much from the 'strength equals defence' assumption) which teaches that nuclear weapons, as the most powerful category of arms, can deter a conventional threat. Equally, nuclear weapons can deter a nuclear threat. But in no way can conventional weapons deter a nuclear threat. There is little scope in these propositions for more detailed formulations of what precise threats the state might be facing. Nor is there any room for the possibility that in modern Europe *any* war at *any* level would be so unpleasant to the West, given what we have to lose, and dangerous to the East, given their internal instability and the threat on the China front, as to be in itself a deterrent to aggression.

It follows from these assumptions that the Government approaches all military dealings with the East on the basis of strict reciprocity. 'The fatal flaw', said William Whitelaw in a public address, 'in the pleasing and plausible façade of unilateral disarmament is that those who threaten us abroad are not the forbearing and kindly souls that we might wish them to be.'[66] Concessions must be exacted from the other side before action can be taken. Multilateralism is therefore the only possible approach to either disarmament or arms control. Unilateralism is not only futile, since it will not be imitated by anyone else, but positively dangerous, since it would upset the military balance, encourage the opposition not to negotiate seriously and negate most of the progress already made in arms control. It would, in short, destabilise nuclear deterrence in its political guise mentioned above. 'Unilateral disarmament is the enemy of multilateral disarmament,' said the Government.[67]

Fourth, arising from this, there has been the repeated assumption that any approach to disarmament must be a negotiation from a position of strength. As a general axiom this is unexceptional, but its pursuance militates against the achievement of any disarmament. For it is not obvious how much relative strength is required before negotiation can be undertaken, and if the other side follows the same sensible axiom, they will presumably not agree to negotiate on such terms. It seems a strange proposition that to negotiate disarmament it is necessary to acquire arms in order to renounce them.

More plausibly this assumption leads logically to the proposition that what is being negotiated from positions of strength is not disarmament at all but arms control: an attempt to stabilise rather than reduce weapons; to curb the rate of increase of costs rather than spend less; to keep military capabilities within a dynamic 'structure' of deterrence or a calculable 'military balance' rather than alter the rules. Despite the severe limitations of arms control over the last fifteen years, this is regarded by the Government as feasible,[68] and it points to its involvement in many international forums as evidence of its intent to conduct 'a serious programme of arms control' as Mr Atkins expressed it.[69] This is the way forward as the Government sees it, and what is listed under a willingness to pursue multilateral disarmament is, in fact, a process of arms control. A substantial success in this would steal a good deal of thunder from the Peace Movement.

Nevertheless, it is impossible to negotiate anything other than arms control under these conditions, and the urge to 'strengthen' is given a higher priority in this axiom than the urge to 'negotiate'. More importantly, it is derived from the premise that the opposition do not have any internal (or indeed any other) motives of their own to disarm. To argue that the Soviet Union will not react to any unilateral disarmament move is to assume that there are no pressures within the Soviet Union that benefit from disarmament.

The 'negotiate from strength' assumption is helpful in other ways, however. It provides an important rationale for solidarity within NATO. It is an axiom, echoed constantly by other NATO leaders, which justifies the Government's policy of trying to maintain the political side of deterrence. It also serves to rationalise an extension of alliance unity into the framework of the European Community. The role of political co-operation within the Community has been stressed as an important foundation of the general strength of the West in relation to the East;[70] a strength that will gain more political importance as the arguments against disarmament are linked with continuing membership of the European Community.[71]

Some of these assumptions are reinforcing, some are contradictory. None of them, however, are beyond challenge, and all of them are examined in some way in the chapters which follow. It is, in fact, not too much to say that disarmament has become a unique issue in current British politics. The Peace Movement is over twenty years old and has never enjoyed so much support. Disarmament has never been discussed in so many other organisations such as trade unions and churches. Political parties have spent more time than ever before debating questions of disarmament. No British Government has responded so strongly to the Peace Movement as the present one. The rise of the Peace Movement has been extremely rapid, and though this may indicate that it could disappear just as quickly, it seems certain to become an electoral issue of some importance. And all this has taken place against the background of a radical upsurge in disarmament sentiments abroad, and a defence policy at home that is facing reappraisals from a number of quarters.

In the light of this debate on disarmament an academic contribution which will explore, inquire and analyse from different points of view the assumptions and tendencies of official policy is essential. This is not to say there are occasions when protest is inappropriate: the exclusion of E. P. Thompson from the Dimbleby lecture was one, and the refusal of the BBC to broadcast an Open University lecture given by Professor Michael Pentz was another. We do not respect the BBC for its handling of public discussion. We are acutely concerned about that discussion. The views of those who criticise official and government policies are habitually misrepresented and distorted; they are often trivialised and evaded. They are, in short, not treated with respect. To describe the contributions made by critics as protest is to diminish them – protest is *mere* protest – it suggests that the critics cannot function on the same ground, the same level, as those they criticise.

The decision made by the BBC to ask Professor Laurence Martin of Newcastle University to be the 1981 Reith lecturer gave us an opportunity to respond on an academic level to the crucial issues in the nuclear arms race debate. These chapters are an alternative perspective; they represent not an opportunity for protest, but for organising an original intervention into public discussion. They assert and demonstrate that within the universities there is a second voice distinct from that of the Government and media establishment. The contributors, from their different points of view, have brought their academic and professional tools to bear on questions which many people find hard to discuss. These lectures express an urgency, a concern for policy, a conviction that policies must change. We hope they contribute to a public discussion which we must now all endeavour to sustain.

Mary Kaldor

Is there a Soviet military threat?

Earlier this year, Caspar Weinberger gave secret briefings to NATO defence ministers on the magnitude of the Soviet military threat. The ministers were reportedly so 'shocked' by what they learned that they asked Weinberger to publish the information. The result is a glossy pamphlet called *Soviet Military Power*,[1] which catalogues, somewhat exaggeratedly, the Soviet military build-up over the last ten years.

As propaganda designed to influence the growing disarmament movement, the report misses the point. Those of us who oppose nuclear weapons do so not because we are not afraid of the Soviet military threat, but because we reject the concept of deterrence as a form of defence, and are afraid that any war in Europe would rapidly become nuclear. Let us suppose that Weinberger's description of Soviet military power is correct, and that the Soviet leadership is as irrational and expansionist as people like Weinberger seem to assume, and that we do in fact face the same situation as we faced in 1938, with the Soviet Union playing the part of Nazi Germany, are nuclear weapons the correct response? Or would they destroy what is to be defended?

One has only to look at the discussion about nuclear proliferation to appreciate the argument. Most of us do not regard the spread of nuclear weapons as a way of containing conflict in South Asia, the Middle East or Southern Africa. On the contrary, we are appalled at the prospect that India and Pakistan, Israel, Libya and Iraq, or South Africa might acquire nuclear weapons and the means of delivery – they would surely be used. If Europe became as unstable as these areas – and it is perfectly possible – the pervasive presence of nuclear weapons could prove a terminal disaster.

We *know* that the Soviet Union is heavily armed, but this is not a justification for a new arms build-up by the West.

The confusion of the two issues – the Soviet military threat and the case for nuclear weapons – has provided a convenient smokescreen for evading the central arguments about disarmament. It is as though the proponents and opponents of nuclear disarmament never listen to one another. They talk at cross purposes. We say that we are deeply afraid of nuclear war; they say they are deeply afraid of the Soviet Union. Sometimes we are drawn into a critique of the Soviet threat and this is used to discredit our position. Whatever we judge to be the likelihood of a Soviet invasion of Western Europe, for this is, after all, what 'they' mean by a Soviet military threat, is actually *irrelevant* to the debate about nuclear weapons.

This does not mean that we ought not to be concerned about the Soviet Union. On the contrary, we need a realistic assessment of all military threats so that we can develop credible alternatives to the present policies of Western governments.

In *Soviet Military Power*, Caspar Weinberger makes no comparison with the United States and NATO. This is perhaps one of the most striking features of the report. Here and there comparisons are made which are, on the whole, reassuring. The Soviet naval infantry, for example, is 'small in comparison' to the US marines. (Actually, the report also says that the Soviet Union has the second largest force of marines in the world. This is wrong. South Korea, Taiwan and Thailand all have larger marine forces.) The Soviet Union still continues to lag behind the United States in microelectronics and in computers, nearly all Soviet models of which are 'copied' from Western models. But the absence of any generalised comparisons makes it difficult to attach a meaning to the listing of weapons, manpower, and expenditure. Indeed, reading the report, one is constantly struck by how easy it would be to substitute the word 'American' for 'Soviet' and make small but appropriate changes in phraseology. Would it sound equally 'shocking'?

The preface would then read;

All elements of the American armed forces continue to modernise with an unending flow of new weapon systems, tanks, missiles, ships, artillery and aircraft. The American defence budget continues to grow to fund this force build-up, to fund the projection of American power far from American shores [the Rapid Deployment Force], to fund American use of proxy forces to support reactionary [instead of revolutionary] factions in an increasing threat to international stability.

Admiral Rickover, until recently the Chief of Staff of the US Navy (instead of Admiral Gorshkov), might have said; 'The American navy is an instrument of a democratic [instead of 'peace-loving'] policy and the friendship of nations [instead of 'peoples'], a policy of suppressing the aggressive aspirations of communism [instead of 'imperialism'] deterring military adventures and resolutely counteracting threats to the security of the free world [instead of 'people'] on the part of the Soviet Union [instead of 'imperialist powers'].'

The description of how military sales have grown into a 'multi-million annual programme', the favourable terms for arms deals, the signing of treaties and the role of military advisers, proxies and intelligence activities all seemed eminently apt; as did the view that Soviet leaders see 'a growing Soviet military strength as providing a favourable backdrop for the conduct of their foreign policy'. The only part that did not quite ring true was the bit about how defence was 'in the hands of a tested political leadership supported by very experienced and long-established staff' and how the Minister of Defence was 'an able and decisive leader'. Perhaps the Soviet Union would say the same thing about the United States. We know that Soviet leaders are absurdly impressed by American techniques of weapon system management and have applied some of these techniques in industry.[2] They might also represent American leadership in a favourable light.

If we compare the figures provided by *Soviet Military Power* with what we know about NATO forces, the military threat from the Soviet Union – the possibility of a Soviet invasion of Western Europe or Soviet blackmail – looks distinctly less menacing. We are told, for instance, that the armed forces number 4.8 million. According to the International Institute for Strategic Studies, this is the number for the Warsaw Pact as a whole.[3] Yet NATO armed forces number 4.9 million people. Moreover, half a million of the Soviet military manpower are construction workers receiving no real combat training, while a further half a million are in the KGB and the MVD internal security services.

We are told that 'the estimated dollar costs of Soviet military investment exceeded comparable US spending by 70% in 1979' (this refers presumably to equipment spending). Now military spending is extremely difficult to assess. There are many different estimates and no real way of comparing them. This statement is presumably based on Central Intelligence Agency estimates. The Central Intelligence Agency has adopted a highly dubious method for estimating the dollar cost of Soviet military spending in which Soviet military equipment (considerably cheaper, simpler and less advanced than comparable US equipment) and Soviet manpower (likewise cheaper and possibly less efficient than US manpower) are valued at the price of their US counterparts. So for instance the MIG-21 may be regarded as the equivalent of the F104 Starfighter, and given the same price. That is a very unrealistic way of making estimates and the result is to inflate considerably the Soviet military budget in comparison with previous estimates. But even according to CIA figures, NATO *as a whole* outspent the Warsaw Pact by $207 billion in the years 1970–9.[4]

We are told that the Soviet Union has 7,000 strategic nuclear warheads. In fact the United States has more than 9,000 strategic nuclear warheads.[5] Further, all Soviet intercontinental rockets are liquid fuelled. The United States abandoned liquid fuel years ago because it was so dangerous and unreliable. The SS-16, an attempt to develop a solid fuel rocket, was reportedly a technological disaster. (The SS-20 medium range land based missile was developed from the SS-16.)

We are told that the Soviet Union has 1,297 surface combat ships. In fact there are only 294 *major* combat ships and this number is declining as the Soviets retire older ships.[6] In contrast the United States has a substantial programme of expansion in major vessel construction. In fact the report reveals that the Soviet Union has only twelve major surface warships under construction compared with forty-two for the United States. NATO forces outnumber Warsaw Pact forces in aircraft carriers, frigates and destroyers by slightly more than 2:1.

We are told that the Soviet Union has 180 divisions in the ground forces. (Soviet divisions are much smaller than Western divisions.) Ninety-seven of these are at less than 50 per cent (an average of around 20 per cent) of their authorised wartime strength. And only forty-six are combat-ready by Pentagon criteria. Furthermore, we know, from other sources that some of these divisions – for instance the 120th Guard Rogachev motorised infantry division in the Belorussian military district, or the 2nd Guards Taman Motorised Infantry Division in the Moscow military district – exist only for show. According to a former Soviet soldier, Victor Suvorov, in *The Liberators*, these divisions[7]

only know parades, demonstrations, solemn visits by foreign guests, guards of honour, and they have no battle training whatsoever. All these 'court' divisions – there are nine of them in the Soviet army – are absolutely incapable of fighting. But they are kept always at full strength, with 12,000 men in each, which represents 108,000 of the very best soldiers and officers in all the Soviet land forces.

A further seven divisions are currently based in Afghanistan, leaving only thirty combat-ready divisions, presumably the thirty divisions available for combat action in Eastern Europe. What happens if there is a war on the Eastern front with China?

As for the equipment of the Soviet land forces, production of military equipment in many categories – self-propelled artillery, multiple rocket launchers, anti-aircraft artillery, tanks – has fallen over the last five years. The Pentagon report reveals that Soviet tank production in 1980 was 2,500. In 1970 it was 4,500. Moreover, so great is the need for foreign exchange that, last year, 30 per cent of these were exported to countries outside the Warsaw Pact.[8] Figures for equipment are also very difficult to estimate. The Pentagon, and other alarmists, make much of Soviet tank superiority. How is this measured? There are various ways to estimate tank numbers, all of which tend to exaggerate amounts. The most usual one is to count the number of divisions and assume a given number of tanks per division, and further assume that every division is fully equipped (which is not the case). Or, it is possible to estimate Soviet tank production, and these estimates have assumed a fairly static rate of production. Yet another method is to count what appear to be tank sheds from satellite pictures and to assume that these are full.

We also have to take into account the fact that Soviet tanks are much less reliable than Western tanks. Also, the Warsaw Pact has a policy of abandoning broken down tanks on the battlefield, whereas NATO has a policy of retrieving and repairing them. Finally, NATO has a clear superiority in anti-tank weapons.

Likewise the costs of readiness – lack of spares, reliability, durability, lack of training, personnel problems, alcoholism, absenteeism, low enlistment – that have plagued the United States army also seem to be characteristic of the Soviet army. There are also said to be problems with homosexuality. (Although I cannot figure out quite why this is a military disadvantage.) Soviet operational maintenance is low. Soviet tank drivers are issued with sledge hammers to help them change gear. The widely touted new T72 battle tank has an automatic gun loader with the unfortunate habit of loading the gunner rather than the ammunition.[9] Also the tour of duty of Soviet conscripts in the Soviet forces in Europe is six months. As a result, so I am reliably told, every six months, Soviet readiness drops to 10 per cent as a new batch of recruits arrive.

The point is that by no stretch of the imagination could the Soviet Union *win* a war against NATO forces. This is even true in Central Europe where, we have been told, not just in the latest Pentagon report but repeatedly for the last thirty years, that the Soviet Union enjoys overwhelming conventional superiority. The case for nuclear weapons in Europe, and NATO's policy of first use of such weapons, has been based on this so-called fact – on the assumption that we cannot defend ourselves from a Soviet conventional attack.

Table 2 shows the ratio of NATO manpower, tanks and aircraft compared with the Warsaw Pact taken from *The*

Table 2 Ratios of NATO and Warsaw Pact manpower and equipment 1971-2 to 1981-2 in north and south Europe

Manpower				Main battle tanks				Land attack aircraft and fighters			
1971-2		1981-2		1971-2		1981-2		1971-2		1981-2	
NATO	Warsaw Pact	NATO	Warsaw Pact	NATO	Warsaw Pact	NATO	Warsaw Pact	NATO	Warsaw Pact	NATO	Warsaw Pact
1.00	1.21	1.27	1.00	1.00	2.80	1.00	1.54	1.00	1.88	1.00	1.35

Source: *The Military Balance, 1971-2 and 1981-2*, London, International Institute for Strategic Studies.

Military Balance for 1971-2 and 1981-2. This is the annual publication of the International Institute for Strategic Studies, which is widely quoted by newspapers as well as members of the defence establishment. In each case the ratios have moved in NATO's favour. The Soviet Union may have introduced new classes of tanks and aircraft, but so has NATO; the new leopard tank, the F14, F15, F16, and Tornado aircraft have all been introduced during recent years. In the case of manpower, NATO now has superiority in Europe. NATO military manpower in Europe is 2.1 million people; Warsaw Pact military manpower in Europe is 1.7 million people. In the other categories (aircraft and tanks) it is still the case that the Soviet Union has numerical advantage, though less than ten years ago.

The 1980-1 *Military Balance* concludes:[10]

The overall balance continues to be such as to make military aggression a highly risky undertaking. Though tactical redeployments could provide a local advantage in numbers sufficient to allow an attacker to believe that he might achieve tactical success, there would still appear to be insufficient overall strength on either side to guarantee victory.

Finally, what of the new Soviet superiority which is so widely discussed today – their alleged superiority in theatre nuclear weapons? This issue provides a prime example of how selective it is possible to be when making these kind of calculations about the military balance. The point is that if both sides are not symmetrical, it is always possible to pick a category of weapons in which one side is superior to the other. The category picked for theatre nuclear weapons is extremely limited. The category that the United States has adopted – which is why President Reagan's 'zero option' looks so curious – is entirely based on a comparison of land-based missiles that can hit the Soviet Union from Western Europe, against land-based missiles that can hit Western Europe from the Soviet Union. It does not include submarine-based missiles and nuclear-capable aircraft assigned to NATO's European command, that can hit the Soviet Union, nor short-range delivery systems that can hit Eastern Europe from Western Europe.

Overall, if we include *all* nuclear weapons in the European theatre, NATO probably enjoys numerical superiority in nuclear warheads assigned to Europe of approximately 5,500–6,500 compared with estimates for Warsaw Pact nuclear warheads which range from 3,500–6,500 – the lower figure being the more likely. But is it any comfort to know that NATO has more nuclear warheads, or bigger ships or more soldiers than the Soviet Union? After all, it takes a good deal less than 1,000 or so nuclear weapons to inflict incalculable destruction. What this comparison shows us is surely that the Soviet Union is nearly as heavily armed as the United States, that the Soviet Union, give or take a few warheads, men and combat ships, is just as deeply involved in a crazily escalating arms race, and this surely should be a distinct cause for alarm.

There is no Soviet threat in Weinberger's sense. We are not in imminent danger of invasion. It is fanciful to suppose that the Soviet Union can 'bend us to its will', unless, of course, the exaggerations and distortions overdo their job and instil in us a sense of fear and overwhelming weakness. It is clear that Weinberger is on a 'threat inflation trip' designed to justify his own arms build-up. There is also no question but that our own media and political leaders exaggerate the Soviet threat. The annual Defence White Paper produced by the British Government is a monstrous distortion of the facts. If anything, such distortions have become greater over the years as the public have become less inclined to believe them. The fact that the Soviet Union has not invaded and that, on the whole, détente has survived has made these kind of distortions much less credible than they used to be.

Having said this it must also be recognised that the Soviet Union has not helped its own case. The Soviets have not denied credibly allegations that they almost certainly could have denied honestly. They have remained secretive, generally refused to provide information, and by this attitude have reinforced many of the more alarmist conclusions in the West.

Why, for example, should not President Brezhnev start the Geneva talks by accepting the zero option? Given the degree of overkill in the European theatre, would it really make much difference if Brezhnev agreed to give up 600 or so missiles, which is what the Americans are asking. His response to the Reagan offer shows that he too plays the numbers game. He has extended the weapons to be covered in negotiations and selectively excluded others. Why do these systems have to be negotiated away? Greater evidence of genuine support for the Geneva talks on both sides would be a willingness to take some kind of unilateral action.

Clearly, there is a threat to peace and stability which stems from the presence of so many immensely destructive instruments of war in both East and West. This is why we need to consider the ways in which the Soviet Union contributes to the risk of war and inquire into the source of Soviet arms build-up.

It is often said that the Soviet Union is acting defensively; with this I would agree. But it does not mean that the Soviet Union will not act in irrational or dangerous ways. Let us consider the risk of war.

Like the United States, the Soviet Union presides over a declining empire. In a recent article in the *Washington Post* J. K. Galbraith describes how he perceived the Soviet empire when he became ambassador to India under the Kennedy Administration, at the height of the American era:[11]

The Soviet Union, incomparably the greatest power in Europe, was united geographically and in political and economic faith and system

*with China, the greatest power in Asia. Along the western marches in
turn was a seemingly faithful band of communist states . . . similarly to
the East, the writ ran on to North Korea and North Vietnam. One
marvels now to think of it: an imperium, as it seemed, extending from
the Brandenburg Gate to the port of Haipong. There had been nothing
like it since Genghis Khan, or as the Russians might prefer Rome
itself. . . . But there was yet more. In Indonesia, Sukarno was backed
by a large and powerful Communist party. Egypt, the most influential
country of the Arab world, was recipient of an increasing flow of Soviet
arms and advisers. As was Ben Bella in Algeria. There was support to
Kwame Nkrumah in Ghana. In Italy and France huge Communist
parties seemed in impeccable subordination to Soviet command . . . more
important was the feeling everywhere in the poor lands that socialism
was on the wave of the future. . . . Moscow not Washington (or New
York) had the custody of the future.*

What a contrast is the Soviet empire today. The Soviet
Union is now encircled by a hostile China and dissatisfied
East Europeans. As Galbraith points out, the evidence for
the new Soviet adventurism is based on intervention[12]

*in Afghanistan to rescue a failing Marxist regime, a country as
inhospitable to imperialism in the last two centuries as any in the world.
And in Angola, where the MPLA regime is sustained by Cuban
soldiers and, in a possibly more practical way, by revenues from Gulf
Oil. And in Ethiopia, where, as Evelyn Waugh once observed, the writ
of governments have never run reliably very much beyond the airport,
in his day, the railway station.*

From the Soviet point of view, Soviet foreign policy could
be said to have suffered a series of major setbacks. It has lost
China as an ally, it faces rebellion in Eastern Europe, and a
military quagmire in Afghanistan. Many of the Soviet
Union's main adventures in the post-war era which looked
so successful (particularly important was the relationship
with Egypt) have failed.

They failed precisely because of the defensive nature of the
Soviet Union. Although one should not underestimate the
quest for control within the Soviet sphere of influence, one
must remember how the Western policy of containment, of
ringing the Soviet Union with military alliances and bases,
must have appeared to the Soviet Government. Soviet foreign policy can largely be viewed as an attempt to try to

offset containment, to cross the defensive barrier, and to reduce the possibility of a military threat to the Soviet Union. That kind of policy was always tempered by Soviet fears of confrontation with the West, and this always restricted the kind of support the Soviet Union could offer to Third World regimes. This was most clear in the case of Egypt. The Soviet Union was so anxious that the Middle East War should not lead to global confrontation that the kind of support the Soviet Union provided for Egypt was very restricted, for instance, the refusal to supply certain types of offensive equipment, and limitations on the numbers of spares. That was the major reason why Sadat expelled Soviet advisers, and the Soviet Union lost a good deal of prestige throughout the Arab world as a result.

It can be argued that there was a real sense of failure, and frustration from the Egyptian experience, and paradoxically a real sense that the Soviet Union had to take greater risks if it was to continue to gain influence and extend support for Soviet policies throughout the Third World. This sense that the Soviet Union could not just withdraw and abandon important interests abroad may have led to a much more aggressive policy. Even though Soviet actions in Afghanistan might be considered by some more justifiable than Soviet behaviour in Hungary, in Czechoslovakia, and now in Poland, it nevertheless did represent an extension of the willingness to use military force. From this perspective the recent so-called 'adventurism' can be seen less as evidence of expansionism and more as the defensive manoeuvres of what Michael Klare has described as the 'Feeble Giant' – a last ditch attempt to recapture the gains of an earlier era.[13]

The Soviet Union has always been very much poorer than the USA and lacks the sophisticated levers of power that have been available to the American Government. Soviet influence in the Third World has largely been limited to offers of arms and military assistance, whereas the United States has been able to provide food, finance, and economic advisers. And within Eastern Europe, Soviet methods have been particularly crude and brutal. The idea that the absence of economic means of influence leads to increasing reliance on military means is also applicable to the United States.

One can see in America's anti-Soviet rhetoric and renewed emphasis on arms, a sense of being squeezed. The United States lacks the economic clout it had in the past; it is no longer able to provide so much economic assistance; it can no longer give arms away – Third World countries have to pay for American weapons and that reduces very much the kind of political influence than can be exerted alongside the provision of arms.

As in the United States, Soviet economic growth has also declined in the 1970s. The period of 'extensive' growth absorbing an increasing amount of labour and raw materials has come to an end. Yet the Soviet Union seems unable to proceed to a period of 'intensive' growth, introducing labour and raw material saving innovations. Indeed, as in the USA, productivity growth has actually been declining in the last ten years. It is also probably true to say, as in the USA, that military spending has contributed to the process of economic decline. Military spending represents a much higher burden to the Soviet Union than to the USA, accounting for around 8 to 14 per cent of its gross national product. Defence production accounts in some estimates for 25 per cent of Soviet manufacturing. Because military technology has become so complex and expensive it is increasingly remote from civilian needs. The absorption of scientists and engineers, the distortion of ideas about technology, may well have contributed to the decline of productivity.

The failure of living standards to grow, in Eastern Europe as well as the Soviet Union, is likely to lead to growing domestic dissatisfaction. In the absence of democratic fora, this is expressed in drunkenness, absenteeism and even the occasional strike as in Togliattigrad. The Soviet state reacts by resorting more frequently to the mechanism of domestic repression. Repression at home and in Eastern Europe is in turn related to military spending and 'adventurism', not only through the old game of 'scapegoat' but also because of the fear, expressed in so much Soviet military writing, that external defeat can lead to internal collapse as it has done often before in Russian history.

Just as American leaders face declining living standards, collapsing alliances, Third World defiance and domestic unpopularity, and seem to be trying to force their way out with the rhetoric of anti-Sovietism and the brandishing of all they have left – their military superiority and their nuclear arsenals – so the 'Feeble Giant' could prove to be an animal cornered by economic decline, foreign policy failure and domestic repression. But in both cases, the resort to militarism could make their problems worse. It could undermine the economy and, what frightens me, it could lead to further risk-taking and adventurism in the Third World and Eastern Europe. This is the real nature of the Soviet military threat – a threat of economic and political instability and hence a cause of future wars.

But the parallels with the USA should not be exaggerated. There are important differences between the two superpowers and these could have important implications for disarmament. So far we have briefly considered the potential use of armaments, now let us discuss the source of armaments. Both countries have powerful 'military-industrial complexes' and these largely determine the acquisition of armaments – the number and types of weapons to be developed and produced. There is, if you like, an autonomy to the arms build-up within each of the superpowers. There are independent domestic pressures for armament which stem from the military and industrial institutions. These institutions were both shaped in the same dominant experience, the Second World War.

Sometimes the best way to consider the arms race is to imagine that both sides are arming against a phantom German army, that has continued to arm in a linear evolution from the past. That could be a much better explanation for the kinds of weapons they buy than the notion that they are arming against each other. There is one marvellous example of this kind of discontinuity which is rather important and has to do with the current debate about theatre nuclear weapons. No one has a tested doctrine about the use of nuclear weapons because their only use was at Hiroshima and Nagasaki. Essentially Western doctrines were grafted on to the theory of strategic bombing of the Second World War which is how our version of deterrence originated. This is why we initially placed so much emphasis on civilian targets – towns and industries. Now the Soviet Union never had a strategic bombing role in the Second World War and the Air Force was always said to be the 'hand maiden' of artillery. It was basically intended to support army operations in which artillery was considered the key element.

Soviet nuclear weapons thinking is very much a continuation of thinking about artillery, which is why medium-range land-based missiles are so important. In fact the strategic rocket training school was originally the artillery training school and the first head of strategic rockets was the former head of artillery. So in fact when the United States and the Soviet Union look as though they are competing with each other, it may be because they were competing against the same enemy in the last war, and so the institutions which now determine the acquisition of weapons were created in a very similar context.

But there are also important differences in the military-industrial institutions in the Soviet Union and the United States, which stem from the differences in social systems. Capitalism is a dynamic system. Investment decisions are made by individual competitive enterprises. Expansion is necessary for survival. Failure to grow means bankruptcy, unemployment, underconsumption and this tendency affects the military sector itself. This is not just because of the political tensions, and indeed the periodic crises, generated by economic decline, the failure to secure outlets abroad and the resulting loss of legitimacy for all elected governments. It is also that competitive enterprises produce arms and must go on producing 'bigger and better' arms for their survival. This is not the case in the Soviet Union. This is an important contrast. Investment decisions are made centrally, the people who got the most resources last year can usually press for the most resources next year. And so it goes on – producing the same mix of products in slightly larger quantities year after year. Individual enterprises tend to be resistant to technological change. This is because their main concern is to fulfill their quantitative plan indicators and this would be disrupted by technological change. Military enterprises are much like other enterprises. Left to themselves they would just go on producing more and more tanks – not more advanced tanks. Employment is guaranteed and individual enterprises enjoy what might be described as tenure. There is dissatisfaction, but there is no possibility of economic collapse as in the West. The main tendency of the system is conservatism.

If there is a dynamic in the military sector it results from the military competition with the West. The military sector is a privileged sector; it can commandeer spare parts and raw materials; it can cut through red tape; its employees enjoy higher wages, better living standards, etc. It is often said that it is the one sector in the Soviet Union in which consumer sovereignty rules. The consumer – the party and military leadership – is preoccupied, as much now as for the last thirty years, with what goes on in the West, with responding to and 'catching up' with military developments in the West. It is worth noting that the United States had led the way in every major military innovation except the test firing of the first ICBM. Even the Pentagon acknowledges that the West has always been ahead in technological innovations. All the technological innovations the Soviet Union makes tend to follow the American lines; albeit at a slower rate, albeit with much greater emphasis on simplicity and quantity as befits the nature of their enterprises.

If this brief analysis is correct, if the technological dynamic in the Soviet military system does stem from the West, then this suggests that if we achieve disarmament we have some chance of slowing down and even perhaps reversing the process of armament in the East. If we continue to arm, the Soviet Union will do the same and militarism, economic decay and repression will play upon parallel tendencies in the West.

So when we say we are afraid of nuclear war, and they say they are afraid of the Soviet Union, we say: yes, indeed, the Soviet Union is very heavily armed, almost as heavily armed as the United States, and this is very frightening. The only way that we can deal with this military threat is through a positive programme for disarmament.

Professor Johan Galtung

Nato and the States of Western Europe: the search for an alternative strategy

My contribution here is to argue that countries today can work towards peace if they want, via a number of alternative, not mutually exclusive, defence strategies. The viability of the different options is examined by comparing the present sad state of affairs with each alternative. It has been my fate to be a peace researcher for the last twenty-five years, a somewhat lonely experience, and it is interesting suddenly to see that so many people are interested in what one has to offer. Why is that so? It is because of the desperate need for alternatives and the hope that people who have been working in this field might have something to add.

The East-West conflict has a specific structure centred on the Cold War, which must be understood before we can discuss peace and alternative defence strategies. I will begin by making five assumptions as to the nature of the Cold War and the East-West conflict. The first point is that I assume the two superpowers both want global domination; the United States in the name of the system called Liberalism/Capitalism, the Soviet Union in the name of a system called Marxism/Socialism. They are both convinced that the world would be a better place if the other did not exist. When you have two strong actors with those convictions around there is an incompatibility which spells difficulty. But that does not necessarily mean that they want to set up a system which is centred in Washington, New York or Moscow. They do, however, want to guide the whole world towards their kind of system or at least pursue the subsidiary goal of preventing the other one from doing so. Second, I assume that they both have some very strong material interests. The material interest of the United States is basically economic, access to strategic raw materials (the United States itself deciding what is strategic), and access to markets. Any country that withdraws from world trade perpetuates a crime according to the United States. The 'open door' policy presupposes a door that can swing only one way, to let the United States in. The Soviet Union does not have that kind of interest; it is not a world economic power. But it has a profound geo-political security interest in its neighbours. There are thirteen of them (fifteen if one counts Japan and the United States) and it is, by and large, a misfortune to be a neighbour of the Soviet Union.

This does not mean that both superpowers intervene on all occasions. They do not intervene if there is a friendly regime, which is stable, and they do not intervene if there is a highly stable, unfriendly regime. They intervene in the periods of instability. Since the Second World War, the Soviet Union has intervened militarily in Hungary in 1956, Czechoslovakia in 1968 and Afghanistan in 1979; 566879 being the number you are supposed to call in Moscow to get friendly assistance if you want it. The corresponding telephone number in the United States is so long that no telephone system in the world is able to accommodate it. Given this situation the advice a peace researcher might give is not very subtle. If you start as a nation try not to be a neighbour of the Soviet Union. And if you have strategic raw materials dig them up and get rid of them as soon as possible! The latter advice is certainly more practicable than the former.

Third, the East-West conflict is strategic. This arises from the first two points, which together produce politically incompatible situations, and the result is a strategic race. The question becomes one of basic strategic advantage; who is in the superior position if a war should break out. Fourth, as a result of this, both superpowers build up internally a military-bureaucratic-intelligentsia-corporate complex. This complex is slightly different in the two superpowers, but, by and large, it serves the same function. It is self-perpetuating, it steers the country; to a large extent it is a slow occupation from within. Fifth, both of them build up a relatively tight alliance system and the major function of the East-West conflict is to keep the allies under control.

If these assumptions are correct, they constitute a fairly

tight conflict package and this then leads to an arms race which in turn fuels and is fuelled by all five factors. Why is it that they do not stop with the capacity for minimum deterrence? As a matter of fact even one 10 megaton bomb on either side and a rocket in a hardened silo, or mobile according to a table of random numbers or something of the kind, or in an undetectable submarine, should be sufficient as a minimum deterrent. So why do they not stop? I will offer five reasons, one corresponding to each of the five assumptions of the East-West conflict.

One: if you are a global power (in the case of the United States) and essentially a regional power (in the case of the Soviet Union) you have to have as much destructive power as possible, because it is part of the syndrome of being a big power. Not to have it means that you are not big. Bigness carries this with it. Whether it is good or bad, it is this which constitutes being a superpower. Two: a superpower can use it for political purposes, in the pursuit of political goals.[1] The United States made use of the threat to use the atom bomb perhaps as many as ten times after the Nagasaki bomb. The Soviet Union has used the threat perhaps three times. So a superpower tells the other side to 'get out or else'. It is not wise to tell that to the superpower on the other side, but rather to the smaller fry, because the superpower on the other side might not like to be told such things. The United States did this for the first time under President Truman in March 1946 when the Soviet Union was overstaying in Iran and the ultimatum was 'to get out in forty-eight hours or else'. The Soviet Union left after twenty-four hours. One reason why they left was because they did not have an atom bomb at the time. They have certainly made up for that.

The third argument is the strategic advantage of piling up rockets and other devices with sufficient yield and sufficiently low circular error probability (CEP) in order to obtain the lethality that is the ultimate destruction.[2] Piling up such force, if one has a sufficient lead, might provide first-strike capacity. The strategic value of the first-strike capacity is of course tremendous, because it can be used for political pressure, and bargaining. It does not necessarily mean that the first strike is used, but it means that it *can* be.

For that reason the other side has to bridge the gap – hence an arms race. Fourth, there is something called modernisation. It is the military-bureaucratic-intelligentsia-corporate complex at constant work trying to refine the instruments. Anybody who is a university intellectual knows perfectly well how difficult it is to stop intellectuals from doing this kind of work. You would have to give them something else they might want to perfect. Fifth, there is the mechanism of alliance control. The most quoted remark of Weinberger and Rogers these days is 'sharing costs and risks'. Sharing risks means having missiles stationed on your own territory. A submarine-launched ballistic missile or a submarine-launched cruise missile may hit the Soviet Union every bit as well as a dozen shared risks. But whereas the Soviet retaliation for the sea-launched one would be against the United States, the retaliation for a Europe-launched one might be against Western Europe; not to mention the pre-emptive or preventive strike that definitely would be against Western Europe.

These five functions are, on their own, important enough to explain the arms race. One may even argue that they *over*-explain it. But it means, unfortunately, that if we cut out two or three of these mechanisms the others will still be there, which means that we are in a terrible mess. We are in a deeply rooted kind of conflict. This has, of course, become even worse thanks to two factors which are also major reasons why we have this big Peace Movement today. There is a clear tendency for nuclear strategy to slide from the deterrent function to the winning-the-war function. And there is an equally clear tendency to slide from the super-power battlefield to the lesser-power battlefield. Let me explain in more detail what a lesser-power battlefield, or as the North Americans call it, a European theatre war, actually looks like.

Imagine we start with a system where you have Big Brother to the left and Bolshoi Brat to the right and Big Brother says that I am going to destroy you if you do something wrong and Bolshoi Brat says the same. It is a strategy called MAD, Mutual Assured Destruction, and there is no doubt that it serves as a deterrent to some extent. But there is in it something highly negative, and even highly

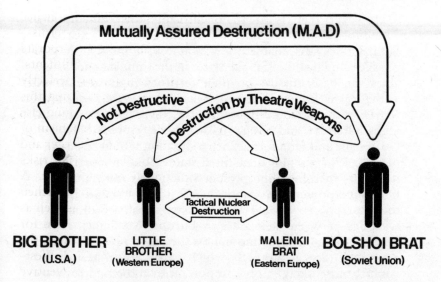

Diagram 1 The changing structure of East–West deterrents

degrading, for the superpowers. For here are Little Brother and Malenkii Brat (see diagram 1) who, when they see the rockets passing overhead, bemoan the fate of the poor super-powers while smugly thinking they are all right. Such a situation is not to the superpowers' liking. I happen to know a couple of very well placed Eastern European diplomats who are of the firm opinion that what really happened during the so-called Strategic Arms Limitation Talks (SALT) was essentially the underpinning of a tacit agreement between the superpowers about a strategic *target* limitation. Namely, is there a way in which the hostage function, the mutual de-terrent function, could be dislodged from superpower ter-ritory, from the heartland, and on to the alliances? If Little Brother and Malenkii Brat in diagram 1 had rockets based on their territory, aimed at the Soviet Union and the United States respectively, then the point of gravity in the nuclear conflict would move away from superpower territory and into Europe. This would not be a hundred per cent solution for the superpowers, but it would at least include their alliance partners in a more substantive role than before, thus deflecting some of the awesome firepower.

However, there is one major difficulty with this solution. The 'Not Destructive' line on diagram 1 does not exist. The Soviet allies are unable to respond with intercontinental missiles aimed at the United States in the same manner as US allies can base missiles on their territory in Europe aimed at the Soviet Union. The only way to achieve a lower level MAD situation would be to give the Soviet Union access to Cuba, Grenada, and Nicaragua and in the future El Salvador, Guatemala and Honduras. Such a situation would be a replay of Cuba 1962; a replay the United States would not permit. As it stands, therefore, the present situation is not quite what both superpowers may want; hence it is not stable. Ideally, the superpowers would like to keep a balance of tactical weapons between their allies in Europe. My hunch is that what is going on at the moment is the piling up of a fantastic arsenal of tactical weapons which make a European based conflict more likely – more important than the middle range 'theatre' weapons.

This argument can most clearly be substantiated by quoting President Reagan. He stated very clearly that he could envisage a limited nuclear war in Europe, with tactical weapons.[3] A couple of days later he virtually repeated this statement.[4] And he repeated it in a peculiar form of English; a form of English spoken by a person who has not been briefed, is speaking spontaneously and relatively honestly, but who is not well enough informed to be more tactical. Had he been properly briefed and learnt the correct phraseology, it would have come out in very fluent, correct phrases and have been utterly dishonest. He simply meant what he said.

Let me add one reason why the Russians have hesitated in stationing so many arms in the Eastern European countries: they might be more afraid than the United States that they could be turned the other way. The reason for that is the basic asymmetry in the situation. The Soviet 'allies' are caught in a geo-political security belt whereas the Western European allies of the United States are not, or less so. They are at the top of the capitalist system, whereas the Eastern Europeans are at the bottom of the socialist one. There is a difference. But that it should be in both the superpowers' interest, by and large, to export the war and prefer a European theatre, I think is obvious. If Norway should ever have a war with Finland we would tend to prefer to have it in Sweden. And if Norwegians and Finns had developed some particularly clever heavy weapons they would certainly ask the Swedes to sign a Non-Proliferation Treaty first.

The obvious question then becomes: what can be done about it? I take as the point of departure that it is only by gradual dislodging from being pawns of the superpowers that we would have a chance of getting out, and surviving. To think and reason our way to an alternative solution, let us now ask the basic question: which are the least secure and which are the most secure countries in Europe? I reject, from the very beginning, the assumption that we are all equally insecure. There is a hypothesis that it is possible to have an unlimited nuclear war in a limited theatre. But this is not a plausible hypothesis; moreover, it acts as a filter for constructive thinking. It is usually a form of thinking indulged in by the extreme military and extreme anti-military to help them to avoid having to answer the following question: could it be that some countries are safer than others? And, if this is the case, what are the kind of policies they follow? And if these policies make sense, could other countries follow those policies? Let me try to be systematic and produce four categories of security for countries in Europe, as shown in Table 3.

Table 3   Framework for an index of relative security of European nations.

Security class	Decoupling from superpower strategy	Non-aggressive policy	Degree of invulnerability	Active peace policy
(high security)				
3				
2				
1				
0				
(absolutely no security)				

The criteria by which countries should be classified into the different security classes are as follows: the first is the degree of decoupling from superpower strategies. Of course, nothing can guarantee security, but it is possible to guarantee insecurity by having on your territory the kind of installation the other side would have to take out, neutralise, immediately. The second criterion is the degree to which a country has a credible non-aggressive defence. 'Offensive' defence weapons would be those which can be used abroad: in other words, anything that can hit the other side; weapons that are mobile, long range and highly effective with a high yield and a low circular error of probability. Non-aggressive or defensive weapons are those which, by their nature, can only be used on home territory. Such weapons would be short range, highly mobile and highly dispersed; such as intelligent rockets that are good at tracking incoming air, sea and land craft and that hurt when they hit. Other examples might be guerrilla defence, or non-military defence; the whole population mobilised to deny the enemy the fruits of occupation. It makes an enormous difference what type of weapons a country possesses, as it is mainly the 'offensive', aggressive weapons that stimulate arms races.

The third criterion is the degree of invulnerability of a country. This is a complex category but concerns the degree to which a country depends upon foreign trade for its basic needs; the extent to which it is centralised; the extent to which its sophistication of technology renders it vulnerable; the degree to which it suffers from class, ethnic or geographical conflicts; and the general state of its morale. The fourth criterion concerns the extent to which a country has a peace policy. This can be defined as the extent to which it makes itself useful in peaceful pursuits; the degree to which a country is more useful to everyone else alive rather than dead. Most countries in Europe have some international usefulness, but often it is outweighed by an aggressive defence policy.

Some interesting implications follow from the act of constructing this table. If the *type* of weapons countries possess is very important, then to judge the military potential of a country only in terms of military expenditure is nonsense. Similarly, it is nonsense only to compare weapons without also comparing the relative vulnerability of the countries. Imagine the situation where two medieval knights were engaged in combat. How absurd it would be for an International Institute of Medieval Studies, located in London, to publish lists of how many lances they each possess, without mentioning that one had armour and the other not. It is vital to take full account of the level of invulnerability. Goliath had much more powerful weapons than David; but also a far greater vulnerability.

A further proposition may be drawn from this: the more vulnerable the country, the more offensive weaponry it is likely to have. For vulnerable countries do not dare have a war on their own territory. Both superpowers are fairly vulnerable. And there is, lurking in the US mind during disarmament negotiations, the fear that the Soviet Union will take a nuclear war better than themselves. The Soviets' notion of what constitutes 'unacceptable damage' does not necessarily agree with the Americans' view. The implications of this are important because they force disarmament negotiators into holding 'fake' discussions. It is impossible to put on the negotiation table the real data because this would reveal that 'we need more offensive weapons than you because we have such a high degree of class conflict in our country, making us more vulnerable.' Knowing some disarmament negotiators, I think I understand some of the differences between what they say and what they think, and the metaphysical nature of their talks. They *have* to construct an artificial world of weapons systems, comparing them one by one.

Having constructed this table of security and insecurity, how can we fit European countries into it? (See Table 4). To begin with, let us consider Switzerland, according to this classification the most secure country in Europe.

The Swiss pursue a defence policy with a logic totally different from the rest of us. The Swiss defence plan of 1973 is one of the most advanced documents in defence thinking that I know, but you almost have to live in Switzerland to know it exists. In essence it consists, first, of total non-alignment and a complete pledge to remain nuclear free. Non-alignment translates into neutrality as a sense of equi-

Table 4   Index of relative security of European countries

Security class	Country	Decoupling from superpower strategy	Non-aggressive policy	Degree of invulnerability	Active peace policy	Total	Cost in dollars per capita
(high security)							
3	Switzerland	2	2	2	2	8	290
2	Finland	2	2	1	1	6	153
	Austria }						
	Yugoslavia }						
1	Greece	1	0	1	1	3	347
	Rumania						
	Sweden★						
	France★						
0	Britain	0	0	0/1	0/1	0/2	376
(absolute insecurity)							

Key
★ France and Sweden are slightly different from the other two countries in this category, but for the sake of simplicity have been included together in this diagram.
0–3 represents the scale of security each country has at present.

distance between the blocs in a conflict. It does not mean that the Swiss are not 'super' Western: they are very Liberal–Capitalist in ideology and system. But it does mean a careful steering between the two contestants. Second, it is Swiss military policy to have almost exclusively defensive weapons, in other words almost no *offensive* weapons. It is Swiss military policy that whatever happens one shall not retaliate against the civilian population of the other side. No such idea, motivational statement, would be taken seriously unless it is seen to be put into practice and the Swiss are rather careful in that regard.

Third, the Swiss pursue a distinct policy of invulnerability. This does not mean Switzerland cannot be obliterated by a nuclear bomb. We know perfectly well that a 10 megaton bomb dropped on Munich under southerly wind conditions may mean the end of a sizeable portion of the Swiss population. But if you are invulnerable you will not be tempted to engage in offensive policies yourself. And the Swiss pursue invulnerability along the dimensions outlined above. They attempt to be self-sufficient in times of crisis, in food, energy, health and weapons. An average Swiss eats 3,200 calories per day and for that reason is slightly rounded. In times of war he will be trimmed down to 2,300 calories and in order to obtain that in a country which is quite import dependent for food, there is a very elaborate plan, and reserves are stocked everywhere to bridge the gap in the meantime. It is a highly decentralised society, meaning that the individual parts can survive even if another part is badly hit, the capital playing a comparatively smaller role in the totality than it does in almost any other European country. It has worked hard to develop a pragmatic, simplistic form of technology in addition to a highly sophisticated and technically competent one. And it is a capitalist country that has bridged class, religion and ethnic contradictions perhaps better than most other countries. Swiss society will not stand up against any brilliant Marxist analysis. It just stands up in fact. In theory it is all wrong, but it works in practice – very much to the chagrin of some of today's Marxists. Out of this comes what you could call a high morale even if it takes a form of *Selbstgerechtigkeit* – of being self-righteous.

Fourth, there is the question of pursuing a peace policy – a policy whereby belligerents would prefer to have Switzerland alive and intact. To facilitate this Switzerland is able to provide banking services, is the headquarters for a number of international organisations, notably the Red Cross, and makes a national industry of being a conference centre. So Switzerland is the safest place in Europe and comes out with the highest score in Table 4.

In class 2 in the table are Finland, Austria and Yugoslavia. They score well on decoupling and non-aggressive defence, though less well on invulnerability because they do not pursue it as conscientiously as do the Swiss. Though, the Final Act of Helsinki was not signed in Finland by chance. It was a systematic, deliberate processing by the Finnish foreign office of other people's conflicts into a product which would also serve their own security.

In the next class are the semi-allies; Sweden, Rumania, France and Greece. France is semi-decoupled by not being militarily integrated into NATO but still being a political member of the alliance – its *force de frappe* perhaps being a NATO force, perhaps not, the level of 'perhapsiness' being decided by the French. On the other hand, the *force de frappe* is highly offensive weaponry. Rumania and Greece are also interesting. They are semi-allies by not being militarily integrated into the alliance. Rumania also has the lowest military budget on the Warsaw Pact side. Greece itself has announced that they want nuclear arms on their territory withdrawn. To be nuclear free means being, in this case, a semi-ally. But Sweden is also a semi-ally. It is not entirely neutral: it is neutral, leaning to the West. A country which relies on the CIA for information as to where it should go with its geiger counter around the grounded spy submarine of another arrogant superpower is not an entirely neutral country. A country that receives the US Defense Secretary with enthusiasm and places its demands for weapons with only that superpower is not an entirely neutral country. If Finland had done the same three things in relation to the Soviet Union, what we would have read then in the press about 'Finlandisation'! There is a certain 'Swedenisation' which makes Sweden half an ally. A higher level of decoupling is the key security factor in all these calculations.

Having constructed this table we can now postulate that, in the case of a war, the most likely survivors are to be found in class 3 and the highest mortality in class 0. What, then, are the costs of this? Using the figures provided by the International Institute for Strategic Studies we can calculate the average defence expenditure, per capita, for comparable countries in the various security classes. The figures are recorded in the last column in Table 4. Disregarding Switzerland, it is clear that not only do countries at the lower end of the scale exhibit decreasing security, but that it is gained at an increasing cost: it becomes a more expensive funeral. The figure of Switzerland is high because it has a long tradition of security, and many of the expenses are of a dual nature, being concerned with the invulnerability factor. The Swiss are able to pursue a perfectly feasible civil defence policy for example – whereas aligned countries find that to implement a civil defence policy would in itself greatly increase tension – thus giving the lie to the belief that alternative defence to nuclear deterrents are impossibly expensive. This can already be seen in conventional warfare. A modern tank costs roughly 500,000 dollars in the cheaper categories; there are those which cost 1 to 2 million dollars. The weaponry needed to destroy a modern tank costs about 4,000 dollars (i.e., the jeep, the bazooka, the intelligent rocket plus a little upkeep for the four soldiers). Now if you have a number of these systems, the tanks will be ineffectual. This is what happened in the middle east war of 1973. An enormous number of tanks were destroyed very quickly by anti-tank weapons. So it may well be that defensive weapons by their nature are less expensive than offensive weapons.

By examining the information in Table 4, we can now draw some conclusions as to what might constitute an effective peace policy in Europe today. A general answer would be for countries to upgrade their security class. If a country is in class 0 it should move to class 1, if in class 1 go to 2, and if in class 2 go to 3, to start with. Let me offer some very concrete ideas on how such movements can occur. I see it as a gradual process in the interests of the country concerned. It can only be brought about by popular movements because the leaders in the client countries are so firmly trapped in the paradigm of the pursuit of squaring the circle. One of the most valuable things in the Peace Movement in recent years has been the extent to which it is almost dominated by women who have this marvellous capacity of not accepting the logic that male experts have developed.

On a very specific and highly political level there are two alternative ways for a country to decouple from a superpower: to loosen ties with NATO, and/or to become nuclear free. One way of loosening ties with NATO is to follow the example of France, Rumania and Greece by continuing political membership, but saying to military integration, 'it depends, it depends, it depends . . .', thereby decoupling the military integration. The model already exists in the activities of the so-called 'protest' countries. How then is it possible to establish a nuclear-free country? I believe in the Alva Myrdal formula. This is the greatest Swedish contribution to peace by any one particular person. Her formula is that the countries who are already nuclear free should make use of a resolution made by the nuclear powers in 1978. Namely that the nuclear powers are willing to guarantee not to attack with nuclear weapons a country that pledges itself to remain nuclear free. For a country that does not have nuclear weapons in peace, like Norway, it involves a declaration that it would not have them in war either. The country then asks the Soviet Union for a pledge that it will not be attacked. It will get that pledge by return mail. They will be very happy to give it. Will they get that pledge from the United States? This is a question of double targeting. Any country is targeted not only from the other side, but also from its own side, since it is possible that a country might be occupied or become unreliable, and in that case something would have to be destroyed on an 'ally's' territory. The United States would have to give that pledge, if only for the sake of appearances. Now, will the pledge be forthcoming from France, China and Britain? I hope that Britain would be kind enough to give the pledge. The French would. The Chinese have already promised that they would give the pledge.

By receiving these pledges the five core neutral countries

would establish a *de facto* nuclear-free zone, one at a time. The moment that the five come together to arrive at a joint instrument it becomes much more complex. One of the key elements is not to insist on a contiguous *zone*. The moment this is done there are years of negotiations ahead, most likely with very little result. So let us now imagine that the nuclear-free area starts with a neutral country, and goes on to the semi-nuclear-free countries, like Denmark, Norway and Greece. If Britain had a government with the same courage as the Greek Government and followed their example this would, in turn, influence Rumania and Bulgaria. Then we would already have a large nuclear-free area.

Next, in terms of alternative policies, it is quite possible for countries to work to an alternative triad of defence. The triad should consist of conventional military, paramilitary, and non-military components. To achieve this a different kind of defence thinking is necessary. Conventional military forces should be highly mobile and highly dispersed; the small units should be relatively autonomous. If you have 100,000 jeeps roaming around with bazookas, never assemble them in one place for a parade! So let us decentralise the army and get the lower ranks of the officers upgraded and the higher ranks downgraded. Let us make the conventional military more like the paramilitary.

The non-military is the part I myself would work in as a pacifist. As a pacifist why do I talk about bazookas and jeeps? I do it for a very simple reason, namely that the line I stand for in my own country will carry a maximum of 10–20 per cent of the population. So I expect that others do not believe in what I believe in, and would see the mix of the three types of defence as much stronger. I think a country that had such a triad would look highly unpalatable to an attacker. If the defensive capacity was sufficiently dispersed the chances of nuclear blackmail would be considerably lower.

Does all of this mean I would expect a war to break out? Not necessarily, but a glance at European history, not to mention world history, makes the thesis that wars somehow, sometimes occur somewhat plausible! Nothing can *guarantee* that a major war will not break out, but an alternative defence policy would decrease the internal motivations to ag-

gression that arise from fear and panic in a crisis, say, to secure food and energy supplies abroad. The more a country is
a client country the less able will its military establishment
be to think in different terms. For the superpowers have done
the thinking for them and their task has been to participate
in staff meetings, US or Soviet training colleges, and so on.
There are however, a surprising number of dissident officers,
even of general's rank, who have resigned, or who are in
retirement, and who have joined the Peace Movement in
Europe, and they are the people with whom one can work.
Those who stayed behind hate them and respect them. In-
terestingly, it is also the case that the people who have
thought least constructively about peace/war problems are
generally the Labour Party and Social Democratic Parties.
There is often among Conservative, nationalist officers more
constructive thinking than among those on the left. This
means that people who do not like each other will sometimes
have to come together on the same committee. There are
surprising bedfellows in the Peace Movement's committee
room. But the world situation is so critical that this might
be one aversion we will have to overcome.

A country must also work to build up its invulnerability
level. It can do so by developing intermediate technology,
decentralised self-reliance and an equitable society. Rather
decent politics, is it not? It means essentially 'green' politics.
Green politics is not what is represented in the political party
spectrum. For that reason it is something much better carried
out today by people themselves. It appeals to local level
politics. To be self-sufficient is the best defence against your
own inclinations, not only against those of the enemy. Finally, more imaginative approaches to the peace policy must
be sought. Countries must study how they can become more
useful to each other; how more symbolic links can somehow
be made without compromising the essentials.

I have tried to indicate that definite and clear alternative
defence policies do exist. They can be carried out unilaterally
by a single country. They do not have to be undertaken by
all countries at the same time. For I do not believe in disarmament negotiations. Quite apart from the metaphysical
nature of these discussions, I do not see any way in which

countries can arrive at the conclusion that they have established parity, take that as a point of departure, and reduce potential destruction levels in any equitable way. I argue with proponents of negotiation in the following way. Imagine they say: 'The Soviets arm to a certain point, we, poor fellows, are less well armed and for that reason we have to arm up to an equal level or surpass it. And then the Russians will admit that this situation is unworkable and both sides will then disarm together.' I always ask the other side: 'Could you please give me your three favourite historical examples of when this situation has occurred; not all, just the favourite ones?' I have never been given one. My next question is: 'Could you give me your *theory* as to why it should occur? Assuming we are not positivists, we do not base it just on data.' Again, no good answer. Finally, I ask: 'If the Soviets are to be so shocked when *we* equal or surpass them in arms production as to want us all to disarm together, why were we not so shocked when the Soviets presumably equalled or surpassed our arms production that we gave in, and we all disarmed together?' I am then told by my US friends that I have misunderstood the whole thing because the Russians are different from us. Then I wonder how the Russians are different? To me the Russians and the Americans seem very similar. Both are driven by the same paranoid, power-crazy and eventually metaphysical logic – and that is where the discussion stops.

But if the European countries do act together, decouple from the superpowers, build up their defensive capacity, make themselves less vulnerable and engage in a peace policy, even the European Community would make sense. That is one way of doing it; but not the only one. The non-aligned countries are our guide in this process and they have come much further and done much more for peace than the alliance countries. Each country can act unilaterally; there is no need to be involved in endless negotiations. Popular initiatives linked to concrete political options can produce viable results immediately. It is along such roads we have to proceed.

Professor Michael Pentz

The threat of nuclear war and the responsibilities of scientists

Three questions arise from the title of this article; 1 Is there a threat of nuclear war and if so, how serious is it? 2 Can anything be done to avert such a threat? 3 In all this, what are the responsibilities of scientists?

The threat

The threat of nuclear war arises in part from the course taken by the nuclear arms race over the past twenty years or so, but much more from the course it threatens to take in the next decade. Incredible as it may seem, there are some theorists who, no doubt nonplussed by the seemingly inexorable momentum of the arms race, have contrived to 'prove' statistically that it does not exist. There are even some academics who appear to take such theorising seriously (see, for instance, Laurence Martin's 1981 Reith lectures). They do not, of course, deny that the numbers of strategic nuclear weapons in the stockpiles of the two superpowers have increased from a few hundred in the early 1960s to over 18,000 in the early 1980s, nor that, if the 32,000 so-called tactical nuclear weapons are added, the combined total of 50,000 warheads has a total explosive yield equivalent to a million times that of 'Little Boy', the bomb that destroyed Hiroshima. It is merely suggested, as does Professor Martin, that there is no evidence that the rate of acquisition [of arms] by one side determines that of the other.

There is ample evidence, however, that the nuclear arms race has followed a fairly consistent pattern over the years. A new development is initiated by the USA and followed a few years later by the USSR. Apart from 'the bomb' itself, examples of this process are: MIRV, the long-range cruise missile; the M-X missile and the Trident nuclear submarine.[1] The initial move is usually justified by claims of a Soviet military threat or an alleged imbalance. George Kistiakowsky has noted, in his book *A Scientist in the White House*, how these threats have been consistently exaggerated over the past twenty years.[2] Recent experience confirms the pattern. M-X was 'justified' by President Carter in terms of a ludicrously exaggerated 'threat' to the Minuteman force from Soviet ICBMs, and in this country, too, there has been a flood of similar propaganda, including some pretty shameless manipulation of the data. As for example, the Ministry of Defence's glossy handout explaining to the residents of Newbury and Molesworth why cruise missiles are not only nice but necessary, is designed to show that the Soviet deployment of SS-20s has created a 'serious imbalance' of theatre nuclear forces justifying the deployment of cruise and Pershing II missiles. The Soviet 'we can do anything you can do' attitude and the US obsession with the notion of 'negotiating [if at all] from strength' have merely accentuated the pattern.

The nuclear deterrent concept is based on the assumption that if both sides have these fearsomely destructive nuclear weapons, neither side would risk starting any action for fear of retaliation. How many nuclear weapons are needed for deterrence? If we had enough to destroy every Soviet town with a population of 100,000 or more, we would certainly have an adequate deterrent – some would say more than adequate. And if the Russians could say the same about the United States then both sides would have more than adequate deterrents for anyone's money. A couple of hundred is the number needed to meet defensive requirements. Why then do both sides have 50,000 of which 18,000 are strategic nuclear weapons?

The first role of a strategic nuclear weapon is called counter-city for obvious reasons – sometimes also called counter-value. Its function is deterrence. The second function is called counterforce and its function is not deterrence. For deterrence does not require large numbers, a couple of hundred is enough. Nor does it require very great accuracy. If someone wanted to threaten Britain by saying 'if you do so and so, I will explode a nuclear weapon on Newcastle,' it would not matter very much if it was aimed with the accuracy of a mile or even two miles. It would still kill most people in Newcastle quite effectively because the explosive power of these bombs is a hundred, or even several hundred times that of the Hiroshima bomb. We do not have any more of a deterrent because we are able to kill everyone in Moscow forty-five times over; once is enough!

The first essential point to remember, is that the quantitative escalation over the last twenty years cannot have, and indeed does not have, anything at all to do with deterrence. The second point that emerges from the first is that the main development over the years has not been in the matter of numbers, it has been an improvement in quality and especially in the accuracy with which these weapons can be delivered to their targets. Suppose the aim is to destroy an ICBM in its silo by launching a missile with a nuclear warhead against it. What can be done to increase the chances of success? With present day accuracies it would be necessary to aim several warheads at the same silo, hoping that one would land close enough to destroy it. How near is near enough? These silos are very well reinforced. A building like the House of Commons would probably be knocked down by an overpressure of between 5 and 10 pounds per square inch. A modern ICBM silo is reinforced to withstand 1,000 pounds per square inch. For that reason, to have a chance, say 90 per cent or better, of destroying a silo, it is necessary to explode a massive nuclear weapon, approximately 200 Kilotons, roughly twenty times the explosive power of the Hiroshima weapon, within about 200 or 300 yards of the target. Otherwise it does not stand much chance of destroying it and it is no use as a counterforce weapon. For the counterforce weapon business, accuracy is everything. One actually gains far more by improving the accuracy than by improving the explosive power.

For those readers who dislike mathematics, let me apologise while I briefly explain why accuracy rather than size is so important. If you do not enjoy maths, do not suffer through the next paragraph because it is the conclusions that are important. It is possible to calculate, and a research paper presented by the Stockholm International Peace Research Institute (SIPRI) has done it, the probability of destroying a single silo with a single warhead.[3] The formula is:

$$P_K = 1 - \exp[-K/2F(H)] \tag{1}$$

where $F(H) = \{Hf(H)\}^{2/3}$

The formula relates the probability that a missile will destroy a silo – the 'kill probability' P_K, to the lethality of the warhead, K, and the hardness of the silo, H. The lethality is related to the explosive power y and the accuracy r by the formula:

$$K = y^{2/3}/r^2 \tag{2}$$

H stands for the 'hardness' of the silo, or the maximum overpressure it can withstand, f(H) stands for a numerical correction factor that depends on H. Note that in equation (2), y is in Mtons and r in nautical miles (1 nautical mile = 1,836 metres).

Equation (1) is valid if the missile system that delivers the warhead to the target area is fully reliable. To take account of missile reliability, the equation needs to be modified slightly:

$$P_K = m(1 - \exp[-K/2F(H)]) \tag{3}$$

Here, m stands for the reliability of the missile. For instance, if a missile is said to have a reliability of 0.8, it means that, on average, for every ten missiles launched, eight will arrive in the target area as expected, and the other two will not, due to some malfunction.

If the same silo is attacked by n separate missiles, each with a reliability m, and each carrying a warhead of lethality K, then the kill probability is

$$P_K = 1 - (1 - m(1 - \exp[-K/2\{Hf(H)\}^{2/3}]))^n \tag{4}$$

It is easy to see that, if n = 1, equation (4) reduces to equation (3); and if m = 1, equation (3) reduces to equation (1).

To be able to calculate any example you like, you need one more formula, the one for the correction factor f(H):

$$f(H) = 0.19/H - 0.23/H^{1/2} + 0.068 \quad (H \text{ in psi}) \tag{5}$$

The mathematically inclined reader will be able to use equations (1) to (4) to verify the main conclusions from this 'calculus of counterforce'. They may be summarised as follows:

(i) The kill probability against a silo of given hardness depends on the lethality, K. The greater the lethality, the greater the kill probability.
(ii) The lethality depends on the explosive yield, y, and on the accuracy r. You gain more from improved accuracy than from higher yield. For example, a tenfold increase in yield increases the lethality by a factor of about 4, whereas a tenfold improvement in accuracy increases the lethality by a factor of 100.[4]
(iii) The kill probability with a single missile can never be greater than the reliability of that missile. This means that as missile accuracies are improved and higher lethalities achieved, it becomes more important to achieve reliabilities approaching unity (100 per cent).
(iv) Attacking the silo with several warheads can considerably increase the kill probability. For instance, if the kill probability for a single warhead is 0.9 (or 90 per cent), the kill probability for three such warheads is 0.999 (or 99.9 per cent). This underlines the importance for counterforce capacity of numbers as well as accuracy.

The example in note 4 (p. 130) shows that the most advanced US ICBM can have a 94 per cent chance of destroying a Soviet SS-18 missile silo. Now you might think that is good; most people when they get a mark of 94 per cent in an exam think that they have done pretty well. Alas, the trouble is that in the counterforce business it does not mean very much unless it is possible to establish what is called a 'credible first-strike capability' which means having a chance of knocking the whole lot out.

The important question then becomes, if there is a probability of 94 per cent of knocking just one silo out, what is the chance of knocking out approximately the one thousand that exist? If you are an experienced punter you will know the answer. If you back a horse at 10 to 1 with £1.00, you receive, if the horse wins, £10.00. If you back on a double and both win at 10 to 1 you should get £100 because your chances of winning are one in a hundred – (1/10) times (1/10). So therefore the chance of knocking out a thousand is 0.94 multiplied by itself a thousand times. The answer is roughly 10^{-27}, or, for all practical purposes, zero.

Now most military thinkers would pose themselves the question and say, 'I am not going to launch a first strike unless I can have a probability of destroying a thousand targets, which is getting on for, shall we say 99 per cent.' The lethality needed to obtain such an outcome would be a K of about 220. Now that is four times better than the best missile in the business at the present time which is the improved Minuteman III. And remember this outcome depends above all on accuracy. If you improve the accuracy by a factor of 2, you improve the K by a factor of 4. Accuracy is the name of the counterforce game. To achieve a 99 per cent level of success an accuracy about four times better than anyone has at the moment is required. If similar calculations were made for the Soviets it would be seen that the Soviets at the moment are slightly worse off than the Americans.

Over the last twenty years deterrence has been abandoned, the numbers have been piled up because the strategy is now counterforce and not counter-city. Accuracy has been improved in the last twenty years – the technological improvements are incredible. Just stop and think for a moment that what has been achieved is the shooting of a rocket outside the atmosphere, letting it go several thousand miles, then letting it spawn 2, 3, 4 or more separate carriers known as re-entry vehicles which re-enter the atmosphere each carrying a nuclear warhead and each aimed at a particular target. Each warhead will then explode close to its assigned target; if it is a Minuteman III it will be within 200 metres of its target. It is fantastic, a technological miracle; but it is not good enough. It produces a kill probability of only 94 per cent which makes a credible first strike as yet impossible.

If we look at what is happening now I can say with complete conviction that the next leap in the nuclear arms race will be the last. It will either be the last leap in the sense used by Lord Mountbatten – a leap into the final abyss of a nuclear war – or it will be the last leap because millions of people in Europe and all over the world have realised what is in store and will have decided to act before it is too late to stop the nuclear arms race and reverse the present suicidal trend. One way or another it will be the last leap.

The changing nature of the nuclear threat

The history of the nuclear arms race as it has been repeated time and time again, is that the Americans are leading the way with the Russians following behind with a time lag of about five to seven years. There are, however, four projects under way at the moment which will change the nature of the arms race before the end of the decade. They are very different from previous nuclear weapons that have been developed because the emphasis is on accuracy. If and when they are developed there will be a drastic change in the rules of the arms race – the race will be over. Let me briefly explain the nature of these four weapons.

The first is M-X. This is a new intercontinental ballistic missile system which is intended to replace the 550 Minuteman IIIs. It is a large missile, similar to the Minuteman III except that it is bigger, and it can carry eight or ten separate warheads instead of three. These are minor factors compared to the importance of the proposal to equip MX with a device known as MARV. MARV does not stand for marvellous, but for Manoeuvrable Re-entry Vehicle, which means that the vehicle carrying the warhead back through the atmosphere towards the target can be manoeuvred. It can be steered. The vehicle can then be equipped with terminal guidance. This simply is a device, carried on the vehicle, which allows it to scan the land as it approaches its target area and to compare what it sees with what a computer carried on board tells it it ought to see. Such a mechanism makes steering very accurate. With MARV a missile can achieve accuracies of around 20 to 40 metres. That is an extra factor of 10 in accuracy, which means a factor of 100 in lethality. If one can assume that the missile system functions reliably, so that the re-entry vehicles gets close enough to the target area for the terminal guidance system to work then this level of accuracy means that the single target kill probability is practically 100 per cent. It is so close to 100 per cent that one can multiply it by itself a thousand times and it is still practically 100 per cent.

This small qualitative change is very important. A change by a factor of 10 alters the whole answer to the question of accuracy. The answer to the question of whether a country has a credible first-strike capacity will, with the arrival of a missile like M-X, change from 'no' to 'yes'. Now any little girl or boy knows that there is a qualitative difference between the answer 'yes' and the answer 'no'. It is not merely a difference of degree, it is a difference of kind.

The second newly developed weapon system is the large nuclear submarine, the Trident. It has a greater missile carrying capacity and a greater range than its predecessors. It has a greatly improved navigational system and a new missile to be called D-5 which will have (guess what) – MARV. It will therefore have the same sort of accuracy as the M-X and the same sort of potential first-strike capacity.

The third new development is the cruise missile, which is a descendant of the Nazi V-1. It is a small, jet-propelled, pilotless aircraft which has a very long range, thanks to having a very modern jet motor, and it is very efficient with certain devices to keep it on course by self-correction when any sort of drift occurs. Not only is it relatively cheap, by missile standards, but it can also fly very low.[5] It has a high penetration of existing anti-aircraft defence systems and anti-missile systems. None of these features, however, are sufficient to account for its enormous lethality. The key feature is its accuracy, which is expected to be better than thirty metres. With this accuracy and with a 200Kt warhead, the lethality K works out at greater than 1,300. With such lethality, the kill probability is 100 per cent, even against a super-hardened silo.

One important additional factor about the cruise missile which is not often mentioned is that because of its characteristics it cannot be included in any strategic arms limitation treaties. It is for this reason that the newspapers in the early 1970s headlined their reports about cruise missiles with 'The Cruise missile, SALT-free and deadly.'[6] This referred specifically to the sea-launched cruise missile called the Tomahawk and made by General Dynamics. It is the ground launched version of this missile that is intended to be put in Britain and some parts of Europe in the next few years. There is an air-launched cruise missile as well (made by Boeing). The US airforce is expecting to have equipped by the middle of the decade some 160 B52 bombers with twenty such cruise missiles each, twelve under the wings and eight in the bomb-bays. Each cruise missile will carry probably a 200Kt warhead: about fifteen times the power of the bomb exploded on Hiroshima. So each B52 bomber will have the equivalent of 300 Hiroshimas on board. They can be launched from the bomber in flight at a distance of at least 500 miles from the perimeter of Soviet air defences. The cruise missiles will fly at an economically high altitude until it is necessary for them to drop down low and they will come in at about ten metres. They can be programmed to change course in a peculiar and confusing fashion so that even if they can be picked up on radar it is difficult to know where they are going. They are, in other words, excellent counterforce weapons with considerable, though not unambiguous, first-strike potential. There is a lot of argument about whether cruise missiles do or do not have first-strike potential since the first generation of cruise missiles are subsonic, and therefore, flying below the speed of sound, may allow an opponent time to react. If, however, they cannot be intercepted by existing air defence systems, and if their destinations are uncertain (to the country under attack), one most likely reaction is to assume that they are aimed at high-value counterforce targets, such as ICBM silos, and to launch their ICBMs before they are destroyed. So, whatever may be the merits or demerits of cruise missiles as first-strike weapons, the dangers of deploying them are all too evident.

The fourth system is Pershing II. This is the army's baby. The US army has been disgruntled for some time because the air force and the navy have got into the nuclear strategic business and they have been excluded. After various manipulations and manoeuvres the army succeeded in joining the big league with Pershing II. It is said to be 'the most accurate missile system in the world'.[7] It is an intermediate range ballistic missile with a range in the region of 1,000 to

4,000Km, depending on the version of missile. It is to be based in Germany. It will be equipped with MARV and so its lethality is guaranteed by its accuracy. It will have a flight time to its target of about five minutes.

All these new developments have one thing in common. They incorporate such high lethality as to make an effective first strike against the Soviet ICBMs possible. It should be noted that, to the military mind, it is not necessary that the retaliatory threat should be reduced to zero. If 'only' 20–40 million deaths result from such retaliation, that may well be 'acceptable' if the opponent's industrial and nuclear war-making capacity has been totally destroyed.

These developments are not, of course, without consequences. The Russians obviously will not simply contemplate the whole of their ICBM force becoming totally vulnerable within the next ten years, and do nothing about it. What will they do? A number of options are open to them.

First, they could put a large number of their missiles on what is called a 'launch-on-warning-posture.' Indeed, the existence of Pershing will oblige them to do this. This means that when their radar as interpreted by the computers warns of an attack the signal goes into the launch systems of those weapons that are threatened. If you are not sure which of your weapons are the target of the attacking vehicle you are in even more of a bind and hence under much more of an obligation to launch them or lose them. The Americans call it the 'use 'em or lose 'em' syndrome. I do not have to elaborate the danger of such a posture; computers are as fallible as people.

A second possible response by the Soviets could occur in a tense situation in which they fear the possibility of a first strike because the other side possess the technical capacity for it. The Soviets might just get jittery enough to attempt a pre-emptive strike themselves to try to destroy as many as possible of these weapon systems as they can so as to limit the damage that will be inflicted upon them. This gives me a particularly creepy feeling being in Britain, because of the very high concentration of top priority targets which would figure in any such pre-emptive strike.

The third option is more subtle and dangerous than either of the first two. The Russians may say that the only way that they can protect their ICBMs because of the American advances is to make them mobile – to shunt them around. After all the Americans were proposing to do exactly the same thing with their M-Xs. The motivation behind such a move is clear. If missiles are moved around, the other side do not know where they are and so cannot attack them directly. If you were very smart you could even move dummies around made out of cardboard and silver paper to confuse the opposition. But if the other side cannot see the missiles they certainly cannot count them. If the missiles cannot be counted neither side will sign strategic arms limitation treaties because it is absolutely crucial to SALT treaties, such as they are, that both sides are able to verify the agreement. We do not have to send spies or inspectors with screwdrivers into the opposition's territory because we can do it all with satellites. With approximately 500 satellites around, surveillance is at the moment very good; certainly good enough to allow both sides to count each others' rockets. If the whole object of moving rockets about is to make it impossible for the other side to know where they are so that they cannot attack them, it is certainly also true that the other side cannot count them. Try counting sheep in a fog on the Cairngorms. It will not work if you have to find the blighters before you can start counting them.

The outcome of this situation will be that once both sides, or possibly even either side, has got a major strategic nuclear weapon system in a 'mobile basing mode' as it is called, then that is the end of any possibility of reaching even an arms limitation treaty such as SALT. Remembering that SALT talks were not even discussing disarmament measures (they are concerned with setting ceilings – and very high ceilings – to the nuclear arms race). Even such limited arms control agreements would not be viable in the next decade and certainly not measures of nuclear disarmament by negotiation.

In this decade four quite different systems are being developed each of which represents a qualitative change from previous developments. Each brings into sight across the horizon the possibility of seriously contemplating a first strike. But how can a first-strike capability exist if one side or the other has nuclear submarines which cannot be knocked out? A retaliatory strike would be devastating, making a first-strike capability unviable again. Not surprisingly, therefore, the last decade has seen an immense effort in anti-submarine warfare research. In this the Americans have a very substantial lead because the key technology is microelectronics where there is a big gap between the superpowers. In fact the developments, even as early as the end of 1979, were so serious that the Stockholm International Peace Research Institute, in its yearbook for 1979, reviewed the developments in anti-submarine warfare and concluded:[8]

*The situation as a whole demands urgent attention. If the USA
achieves a first-strike capability against Soviet ICBMs, as appears to be
one of the objectives of the MX programme, and if this is coupled with
maintenance of the present lead in ASW (anti-submarine warfare), there
are serious grounds to fear that the concept of mutual assured destruction,
with all its faults, will be abandoned in favour of a war-fighting and a
war-winning strategy.*

This situation is compounded by the fact that communications systems for missile submarines are becoming more and more vulnerable, and this applies especially to the Soviet fleet. As a result, there are now some doubts about whether a retaliatory second strike by missile submarines can be relied upon. This increases the risk of a pre-emptive first strike by the USA.

The recent developments in nuclear weaponry have therefore made the concept of fighting a nuclear war and winning, whatever that may mean, a reality and it has been called all sorts of fancy names like 'limited nuclear war', or 'flexible options', or 'controlled escalation' – some sort of atomic tennis played by fixed rules with fixed boundaries.

The continued escalation of the nuclear arms race between the superpowers is increasing the danger of 'horizontal' nuclear weapons proliferation – the spread of nuclear weapons to more and more countries. The only barrier to this proliferation is the political one of the Non-Proliferation Treaty. But adherence to this is impeded by the failure of the principal nuclear powers that are signatories to the treaty to implement Article 6, which lays upon them the obligation to take effective measures towards nuclear disarmament. We are thus confronted with developments, which if they are allowed to continue, threaten to make the nuclear arms race unstoppable and hence irreversible. Since all these developments are well under way, we have very little time if we are to have any hope of stopping the arms race before it is too late. The danger is therefore acute.

What can be done?

The Final Declaration of the United Nations General Assembly adopted unanimously at the Special Session on Disarmament in 1978, is explicit about what must be done:

Removing the threat of a world war – a nuclear war – is the most acute and urgent task of the present day. Mankind is confronted with a choice: we must halt the arms race and proceed to disarmament or face annihilation. . . . The most effective guarantee against the danger of nuclear war and the use of nuclear weapons is nuclear disarmament and the complete elimination of nuclear weapons.

Considering the priorities for disarmament, the Final Declaration unequivocally states that nuclear disarmament must be the first priority.

If we accept these propositions as manifestly correct, there remains the question: how do we get there from here? There has been *talk* about nuclear disarmament for many years, but progress has not been nil – it has been negative. A major new initiative is needed to break the deadlock, an initiative that is itself a practical step towards disarmament. It is probably unrealistic to expect either the USA or the USSR to take such a step. The position of Britain is, however, unique. We were the first to start the process of 'horizontal proliferation' – the spread of nuclear weapons beyond the two nuclear superpowers. The purely military significance of Britain's withdrawal from the nuclear arms race would be small compared with its political significance. Nuclear disarmament by Britain could be the decisive factor in breaking the log-jam of international negotiations, especially if it were combined with political initiatives in Europe, aimed at establishing and extending nuclear-free zones and at the balanced reduction of forces, both nuclear and 'conventional', in Europe, leading eventually to the dismantling of both NATO and the Warsaw Pact.

It seems to me that the case for unilateral nuclear disarmament by Britain can be made entirely in terms of the imperative and urgent need to achieve progress towards multilateral disarmament. That it would also increase our national security and make Britain a safer place to live in, by removing us from our present status as a top-priority nuclear target, is an additional bonus.

Responsibilities of scientists

In this grim situation, what are the responsibilities of scientists? There are two senses of the word – one causal and the other moral or social. Is it 'all the fault of the scientists – after all, they invented these weapons'? What should scientists do to help avert the danger?

In an article in the *Proceedings of the American Philosophical Society*,[9] Lord Zuckerman criticised the fundamental irrationality of the nuclear arms race. He blamed it on the scientists and technologists who have

succeeded over the years in equating, and so confusing, nuclear destructive power with military strength. . . . The men in the nuclear weapons laboratories of both sides have succeeded in creating a world with an irrational foundation, on which a new set of political realities has in turn had to be built. They have become the alchemists of our times, working in secret ways which cannot be divulged, casting spells which embrace us all.

A similar theme has been developed by Frank Barnaby, former director of Stockholm International Peace Research Institute (SIPRI). In his foreword to the 1981 *SIPRI Yearbook*, he writes:[10]

Because of the huge resources devoted to it by the great powers, military science, an activity now essentially out of the control of the political leaders, has succeeded in developing weapons which will be perceived to be more suitable for fighting a nuclear war than for nuclear deterrence. Unless military science is brought back under political control *there is an increasing risk of a nuclear war which, in the words of a recent UN report, would be the 'ultimate human madness'. (My emphases.)*

In his lecture to the British Association for the Advancement of Science at York in September 1981, Frank Barnaby reiterated the point that the nuclear arms race starts with 'the men in the nuclear weapons laboratories. . . . The main reason why (reluctant?) political leaders are changing their nuclear policies is the development of new nuclear war-fighting weapons by military scientists.'[11] Barnaby supports his argument by showing that in 1975–6 over half a million scientists around the world were engaged in military research and development. This figure represents about 40 per cent of all those who are engaged in any research and development and if only physicists and engineers are counted that becomes 50 per cent. The figures are probably even higher today. For example in the United States 75 per cent of all government research and development and one third of all research and development is military. An interesting comparison in this respect is Japan where only one thirtieth of all research and development budget is spent on military research. In the UK over 50 per cent of government research is military. We have over 40,000 scientists and engineers in this country working on defence research and development.

It seems to me that, though the figures speak for themselves, the propositions of Zuckerman and Barnaby are gross oversimplifications of a complex interactive system with several feedback loops. One need only ask who funds the military research laboratories, or the highly organised arms industry lobbies, or the captive mass media, to become aware of some of the interconnections. Barnaby is right to talk about an 'academic-bureaucratic-military-industrial complex', but the word 'complex' needs underlining, and it surely is wrong to separate it from politics and the politicians, as he does: 'the nuclear arms race is now totally out of the control of political leaders.'

The need is not to bring military science back under the control of the political leaders, but to bring the whole complex under the control of the *people*. Barnaby makes this point himself, in the penultimate paragraph of his lecture:

What we must do is mobilise public opinion (and, here, the scientific community is obviously a key element) sufficiently to convince the political leaders that they will not be re-elected or stay in power unless they stop the nuclear arms race.

The scientific community is a key element, not only in helping to *mobilise* public opinion, but also, and more particularly, in ensuring that the movement for disarmament is adequately equipped for its task. At every level there is an acute need for objective, reliable information and advice. As the power of the Peace Movement forces the issues of nuclear disarmament into the arena of public debate, Members of Parliament will increasingly need the expert advice of scientists in preparing their questions and interventions. At the local government level, official propaganda for 'civil defence' (which is, of course, a necessary corollary to the current strategic theories of nuclear war fighting, for which the notion of 'survival' is essential) exposes councillors to pressures which they are, in general, ill-equipped to resist. The Peace Movement at all levels is continually confronted with issues that are often highly technical, and on which it is relatively easy for the apologists of official policies to create confusion and mislead people, provided that they are inadequately equipped with independent information.

On one level, then, we are fighting an information battle and scientists can play a very important role here. A good example is the need to counter the Government's present propaganda from the Ministry of Defence at Molesworth and Newbury (where the cruise missiles will be sited if the Government gets its way). The Ministry has issued a very glossy pamphlet with a rather sexy and somewhat inaccurate impression of a cruise missile on the front cover. It is difficult to tell what it is until one reads the small print and sees that it was made by General Dynamics, and that must mean, to the few who already know, that it is supposed to be a Tomahawk cruise missile. Above the picture it says, 'Cruise missiles', and below it says, 'A vital part of the West's life insurance.' How ridiculous can they get; where, might I ask, and when, do we start collecting this life insurance? Inside the pamphlet there is similar rubbish typified by a set of charts illustrating different quantities of weapons. The colours are pink and blue – nothing of course to do with baby clothes. The pink represents the Soviets' weapons and the blue represents NATO's. On one side of the chart it lists in pink, for 1979, 530 Soviet weapons called SS-4s, SS-5s and SS-20s. On the other side NATO has none. Now even the thickest person in Newbury would get the message; the West is at a disadvantage and we must do something about it. The small print in the booklet tells the reader that cruise missiles will remedy this situation. How do the Defence establishment contrive this? The simplicity of their argument is persuasive and the figures are true, which is the hallmark of a good lie. *But* the title of the chart is 'The balance of long-range, land-based theatre nuclear forces'. They have done it very nicely. First they have chosen a range that is just above the range of Pershing I and so it does not have to be included in the table. Second they have included in the chart only land-based missiles. If they had included sea-based missiles they would have to add a bit to the pink column, because the Soviets have four or five old submarines in the Baltic, but they would have had to count the five Poseidon submarines based in Holy Loch which carry eighty modern missiles, which would take the blue column off the top of the paper.[12] The whole propaganda game is based on twisted examples of this kind. It relies upon ignorance and lack of information on the part of ordinary people.

These considerations have led the recently formed scientists' organisation, Scientists Against Nuclear Arms (SANA) to see its primary role to be that of a 'tool-making' kind – to make the tools needed by the Peace Movement.[13] The emphasis is accordingly on the formation and coordination of working groups of scientists based in universities and localities, producing fact sheets, briefing notes, speakers' notes, articles in the press, pamphlets, books and other materials, primarily for use by the Peace Movement. SANA does not see the primary responsibility of scientists to be that of a campaigning activity aimed at influencing the political process directly. It believes that our hope of ending the nuclear arms race and avoiding annihilation lies in the potential strength of the Peace Movement, of public opinion, providing that it is mobilised and equipped. SANA exists to organise and coordinate the efforts of scientists, both natural and social, to serve the mass movement of the people for peace.

The Right Reverend Dr John A. T. Robinson

A Christian response to the arms race

When I chose this title it did not occur to me that I should need to justify both parts of it. Yet I could hardly believe my ears when I heard Caspar Weinberger, who with the rest of President Reagan's travelling troupe has been doing more than anyone else to orchestrate the European disarmament movement, say recently on the BBC: 'There is no arms race. There can't be. For you can't have a race with only one entrant – and we've never competed.' Just who do they think we are, to believe that – and actually have the nerve to accuse us of being dupes of Soviet propaganda?

Then in an interview to *The Times* before his Reith lectures Professor Laurence Martin, for whom I have a much greater personal regard, was reported as saying: 'The very phrase "arms race" is a bad metaphor; it is neither fast enough nor competitive enough to be a race, and it is not the heart of the problem.'[1] Just how much faster or more competitive has it got to get? And what goes deeper to the heart of the problem?

But I should like to concentrate on justifying my choice of the first part of the title: 'A Christian response', for I am not claiming to present *the* Christian response. There are, and will continue to be, differences between Christians on this as much as on any other highly technical, as well as deeply moral, issue. This is neither surprising nor shameful. There have always been pacifists and non-pacifists in the church, as today there are both unilateralists and multilateralists. And I would plead strongly, here as elsewhere, for a both, and not simply for an either/or. For the line between them goes right through the middle of myself.

On the basic moral issue Christians should be completely at one. At every Lambeth conference over the past fifty years the statement has been reaffirmed that 'war as a method of settling international disputes is incompatible with the teaching of our Lord Jesus Christ.' And there would be unanimous agreement among moral theologians that unrestricted nuclear warfare could never be justified under the doctrine of the 'just war' (a doctrine which may still have important things to say about the 'just revolution' and lesser dilemmas); for it can never meet the requirement of proportionality of response. That for me carries the further corollaries, that limited nuclear war could never be justified either, since one can never be sure that it would not lead to the other, and second that all weapons of mass destruction, whether nuclear, biological or chemical, are out, *even* if one does not intend to use them. For to threaten their use for deterrence is equally immoral if you mean it and foolish if you do not. Unlike Mr Francis Pym when he was Minister of Defence, I could not say that I should myself be ready to press the button. And this is no theoretical issue, for we are requiring young men, in our name, to take upon themselves the terrible burden of this decision. We have one young man, still only an undergraduate at my college in Cambridge, who was one of three key-holders on a Polaris submarine, until he got out, scarred by the experience for life.

Yet I do not want to use my time discussing the issue of whether or under what circumstances the use or threat of nuclear weapons could ever be justified. I am more concerned with how we *stop* them being used. And on this the record of Lambeth conferences or Papal encyclicals is about as discouraging as that of disarmament conferences or arms-limitation talks. They seem to make not the slightest difference. All things go on as they have been from the beginning, except that the arms race constantly escalates and proliferates, the doomsday clock ticks nearer to midnight, and the cry goes up, 'How long, O Lord?' Yet the cry is perhaps the most significant thing. For the breaking of the mould is suddenly beginning to look a real possibility, and the perception is dawning that we *need* not go on like this.

As in British politics, what seemed before so set is cracking before our eyes. The mould of the two-party system is breaking up. That in itself does not *solve* anything, nor does it mean that we should all go off and join the equivalent of the SDP. Indeed the noises I hear coming from the SDP on disarmament are still so uncertain that I need to be much more convinced by them on this issue. Nor is fissiparation in itself a good thing. In fact I have said in effect to Tony Benn and Shirley Williams and David Steel 'I love you all. You represent bits of my deepest convictions. Why can't you get together?' But I know that this is politically impossible, and there are deep and genuine divisions. Yet I am all for holding opposites in tension and convinced that truth comes from both ends at once, rather than from an either/or polarisation or a soggy centre. In any case the lines of division and polarisation are, I believe, largely – and in the time we have got – dangerously irrelevant. And this applies to both the old and the new lines.

The old pacifist/non-pacifist debate has largely been by-passed by recent developments. This does not mean that there are not fundamental issues involved – of how to meet evil or on the place of restraint – on which we shall all come down on different sides at different points. But the old crunch-question of whether to bear arms or accept the draft is increasingly irrelevant. The issue today, I believe, is recognition of the right not to support the arms race with one's taxes. And as a non-pacifist I would want to give my backing to the peace tax campaign, to allow anyone the freedom of conscience, not to evade the burden of taxation, but to divert to a 'peace tax fund' administered under the government for specific peace-making purposes, the proportion of tax allocated to a defence strategy based on nuclear weapons. I believe we must press for this right to be recognised legislatively on the same grounds and with the same safeguards as conscientious objection to military service. It is of course hopeless to expect this present administration to recognise it, and I believe it is a legitimate goal to seek some commitment in this direction from the competing political parties at the next election. And until this freedom is granted it is important to fight for it, and if necessary to go to prison for it, as Bertrand Russell did in the First World War. Yet as a non-pacifist I also want to press for an alternative defence policy that is both credible and usable, which may, initially at least, be no less costly. So again I am split. I will fight for the freedom, but might not wish to go all the way in availing myself of it.

But not only is the old pacifist versus non-pacifist divide anachronous but increasingly, it seems to me, the new line-up between unilateralists and multilateralists is unreal and distortive. And it allows the establishment to divide and rule, as St Paul played off the Pharisees against the Sadducees.[2]

The unilateralists can be labelled 'softies' or neutralists, if not fanatics or freaks, who march with their hearts and not their heads. They can be represented as 'copping out', throwing away the deterrent, upsetting the precarious stability which has preserved the peace, and in effect though not in intention making war more likely. The multilateralists, on the other hand, can be represented as not doing anything till the other side does, as re-arming in order to disarm (alias 'negotiating from strength'), and in effect just fuelling the arms race. So the sterile debate goes on, and no one wins – except the industrial-military complex.

I believe we must all be unilateralists now – and multilateralists. 'Protest and survive' and 'negotiate and survive' are not alternatives. As the latest production of Bradford University's School of Peace Studies, *As Lambs to the Slaughter* (which can certainly not be construed as an argument for doing nothing), insisted the long patient process of dismantling fears, building up confidence, retaining a balance stage by stage, cannot be bypassed or despised, *if* the actual object is to get the powers to remove missiles as opposed to making ourselves feel good.[3] In E. P. Thompson's words at the close of the 1981 Hyde Park rally, 'We've won the argument, but we haven't even stopped one missile in its tracks.'

Perhaps I may be allowed to utter a few fraternal home-truths about how unilateralists look to the other side with whom I am also closely in touch, particularly from where I am placed at Cambridge, within both the scientific and the religious establishments. It is so fatally easy to be counter-productive as, for instance in my experience, are the Israelis to almost all visitors from the West, who go with most of their contacts and sympathies on the Jewish side and return with a far greater appreciation of the Palestinian cause. And it only increases the counter-productivity then to be labelled anti-Semitic, which is about as neurotic a reaction as dubbing nuclear disarmers anti-American.

Now the effect, though not of course the intention, of the self-styled Peace Movement is often as alienating. Are those not wearing CND badges *ipso facto* part of the 'war movement'? A letter appeared in the *Guardian* (I am ashamed to say from a department of theology) just after the Hyde Park rally deploring once more 'the deafening silence of the church' and asking where were all the bishops and clerical collars (who would want to wear one in Hyde Park anyhow?).[4] It went on: 'Enough of this armchair soliloquising! Let the clergy and the leaders of the churches get out of their cloisters and put their feet where their mouths are!' Even if this were a just criticism, and even if putting one's foot in one's mouth were a desirable posture, I would beg those who say such things to realise that they are being about as counter-productive as the Reagan Administration or the Home Office's pamphlet *Protect and Survive* have been on the other side.

The situation is going to be changed – and if we are not in it for this we had better get out – only if the centre of gravity of the great inert body of middle opinion, of leaders and of led, is shifted, albeit marginally. And for that a massive combined operation is going to be necessary, starting at both ends at once. Let me give an illustration which I think is paradigmatic. One of the most successful campaigns of modern times was that which stopped in its tracks the South African cricket tour of England in 1970 – and all such official exchanges since. This was achieved by the combination of two pressure-groups, working from opposite ends. There was the radical action group under Peter Hain threatening to put tin-tacks on the pitch. But there was another group under David Sheppard, then my successor as Bishop of Woolwich, who as a former captain of England and a member of the MCC operated from within the Long Room at Lord's. I don't believe that either alone could have stopped the tour. But together they won the day by giving a decisive tilt to the establishment.

It so happened that just as I was writing this a letter came through my mail asking that 'the teaching staff of the Faculty of Divinity in the University of Cambridge declare their opposition to the presence of all forms of nuclear weapons on British soil and their commitment to a policy of unilateral nuclear disarment.' Would that most of them individually might; but I had to oppose it as simply bad politics. It is rather like asking the Regius Professor of Divinity or the Archbishop of Canterbury to put tin-tacks on the pitch, and when they won't – or they don't answer – accusing them of 'deafening silence'. It is not only inept but actually sets the cause back. I am all for working on both of these characters, and I am all for the mass demonstrations and the pressures from below which are vital to changing the atmosphere and altering the terms of the debate. For I am appalled by how many of the ecclesiastical and even more of the scientific establishment who are still apparently unappraised of the issue or unsparked by it – though as always in any profession this applies less to the genuinely big men at the top than to the mass of second-class minds, especially when research-grants or contracts are directly or indirectly involved. I believe that a great deal has to be done – as is being done, for instance, within the medical profession – to help scales fall from the eyes; and I can testify to how long it took for me really to *see*.

But let us tackle it with both 'valour and discretion', and above all do not let us wantonly divide or alienate our forces. Let me offer one other example, as an awful warning – the case of Rudi Dutschke, the German student activist of the sixties. He was the victim of a bomb-attack (in church) which all but killed him and stopped him either reading or writing for a long time. With great courage he gradually fought his way back to health and got himself admitted to do a PhD at Cambridge, on the understanding that he was completely out of active politics. But a witch-hunt started for deporting him as a danger to the peace. There was massive protest at this from the university, and, for once in those heady days of student riots, everyone was united from the vice-chancellor down to the students. But what did the students do at their mass-meeting? They called a strike, thus hitting not the Government (who in the person of Reginald

Maudling as Home Secretary needed all the battering he could get), but the university, thereby gratuitously setting the students against the lecturers. So despite being torn to shreds by Michael Foot in the Commons debate, to which I listened, the Government won the vote (though certainly not the argument) and deported him to defenceless Denmark, who were honoured to have him, and where I later met him again before his tragically early death. So let us learn the lesson and draw some conclusions.

First let me say something about ends, and then about means. Let me put the object of the exercise like this. The inexorable appetite of the arms race is fed by a process that starts with the research scientists and the hardware technologists (whose salaries of course are already fed by the process), who scan the frontiers of what it is possible to develop, if they are given the resources. They then talk to the military-industrial complex, who don't need much persuading that it must be developed, to forestall the other side and to maintain employment (and of course profits). So the Pentagon talks to the politicians, or Whitehall to Westminster, or the equivalent within the corridors of the Kremlin, and they quickly discover the current missile gap. Finally the politicians, abetted by the media persuade the people to elect them when this is necessary, or work away behind closed doors when it is not. So the M-X missiles and the B1 bombers and the neutron warheads and the Chevalines and the Tridents and the cruise and the Pershings and the SS-20s, etc., etc., are designed and delivered, with ever more sophisticated weaponry waiting in the pipe-line to tease the scientists who talk to the military who talk to the politicians who talk to the people who pay for the house that Jack built.

All we have to do (all!) is to reverse that process: to insist that it is the people who instruct the politicians, who instruct the military, who instruct the scientists what *we* want for *our* defence. It is as simple and as seemingly impossible as that.

Now if you want to move the world the first thing you need is a fulcrum: you have got to get some leverage somewhere. And that is why, because no one individual can do everything, I have decided to put my little weight behind the movement for European nuclear disarmament. For

Europe is clearly the most sensitive and vulnerable spot in the superpowers' armoury. A nuclear-free Europe, or at least a nuclear-free zone (or zones) in Europe, looks like an idea whose time, at last, may have come. For it is no new idea, going back to the Rapacki Plan from Poland in the 1950s.[5] And it is an idea that involves both unilateral *and* multilateral action on *each* side. Yet it has got to be taken beyond slogans by some very hard thinking and tough negotiations. To quote again the authors of *As Lambs to the Slaughter*, it involves deciding the basic question of what is Europe. As they recognise, the slogan from 'Poland to Portugal' will be criticised as grossly unbalanced by the West. 'It will involve removal of all NATO tactical and theatre weapons *and* the much longer-ranged French, British and American systems which are essentially part of the strategic arsenals, while leaving Soviet weapons untouched.'[6] But equally the other zone that is canvassed, from 'the Atlantic to the Urals', 'contains perhaps 40 per cent of all Soviet ICBMs and the base for around 60 per cent of their missile-carrying submarines. In this case the balance, such as it is, has swung the other way and Soviet opposition will be fierce.' But this is no reason for abandoning the vision. It is a reason for requiring as much hard knowledge and hard thinking on the so-called Peace Movement's side as on the so-called strategists' side, and for real dialogue between them.

This is the lesson I believe to be drawn from the welcome offer by President Reagan of the so-called 'zero option' in Europe. First, it would never have happened without the groundswell of protest in Europe against accepting the new American weapons: it shows how public opinion *can* change things. Second, the initial Soviet response must not be regarded as their last word or proof of their perfidy. For what does the zero option mean? Not, as might be thought, no nuclear weapons on either side; but rather 'You dismantle the SS-4s and SS-5s and SS-20s you've installed and we won't introduce the others.' No mention of removing the forward based systems of nuclear bombers and submarines to which these were the response and which can hit the USSR itself, as the SS-20s cannot hit the USA. So a great deal of hard bargaining remains to be done. And the pressure

must be to keep *both* sides to it, not to mention pressure on
our own Government and the French who have so far offered
no independent initiative. So I hope that the upshot of the
1981 Reith Lectures and the Alternative Reith Lectures will
be to bring both approaches closer together rather than far-
ther apart.

One thing of which I am increasingly convinced is that
both sides must get together to produce a strategy for
alternative defence. There is no doubt that one of the dis-
suasive features of unilateralist propaganda, and indeed of
the disarmament movement generally, is that it comes across
to most people as purely negative. I was first appraised of
this by a radical campaigner in the United States who sensed
acutely the effect it was having. It makes the ordinary citizen
feel he is just being left naked and defenceless. That is why
another aspect of the current campaign in which I am interested is the Alternative Defence Commission set up by the
Bradford School of Peace Studies to plan, to put it simply
for a better shield rather than a bigger sword, which need
not threaten anyone or provoke escalation.[7]

The real trouble at the moment is that we have a defence
policy which we cannot implement without committing
suicide, and therefore no credible defence policy at all. This
applies both at the tactical and at the strategic level. At the
battlefield level nuclear weapons are so implicated in a
NATO response to conventional attack that it is impossible
for us in the West to say that we will not be the first to use
them. This is morally, ideologically and tactically a disas-
trous weakness, quite apart from being a most dangerous
trigger to Armageddon, in blurring and lowering the nuclear
threshold. We must extricate ourselves from this position
with all deliberate speed.

At the strategic level, we are equally being propelled into
a first-strike policy, and the shift is not being honestly
acknowledged by our political masters. We are still assured
that the only reason we have these weapons is deterrence,
and that, of course, there is no intention of actually using
them. But the counterforce rather than counter-city strategy,
publicly acknowledged by Carter's Presidential Directive 59,
but implicit well before that, has introduced a new and

dangerous situation.[8] It can be dressed up indeed as morally more acceptable, since the missiles are targeted not on civilians but on launching silos, though since these are in populated areas the destruction and fall-out would still be massively indiscriminate. But what is the point of hitting empty silos? You would have nothing to fire at, nor, since the other side is poised to do the same, to fire with, *unless* you strike first.

This point is powerfully made by Robert C. Aldridge in his book *The Counterforce Syndrome*.[9] Aldridge was intimately involved in designing new weapons systems for the US Government and the technical sophistication of what he tells us is planned or possible reads like science fiction. He got out because he realised what he was being asked to design for. This was no longer to deter, so that the weapons would not be used, but to press ahead in the race to use them first. 'The only possible reason,' he says, 'for developing a counterforce capability is to acquire the capacity to launch an unanswerable first strike against the Soviet Union' – which involves knocking out *all* possible retaliatory second strikes. He believes that this could become a feasible reality by the mid-1980s – that is, for the United States; the Soviet Union has not a hope. The deadliness of the newer missiles, like the Trident and the cruise missiles depends not on their size but on their pin-point accuracy. They are essentially first-strike weapons: for retaliation the old would be adequate to 'overkill' many times. And what, one may ask, does Britain want with an independent first-strike capability? Under what conceivable circumstances can we imagine it being used?

In fact the Trident programme for Britain seems about the most egregious abuse of public money that it is possible to conceive. One thing – and it is about the *one* thing – on which Mr Healey, Mr Benn, Mr Owen and Mr Steel are agreed is that they would cancel Trident. Under any conceivable alternative government it will go down the drain, and meanwhile contracts are doubtless being negotiated containing indemnity clauses against cancellation which will cost us millions – all for nothing. If Mrs Thatcher is *really* concerned to cut public expenditure, here is where she should start.

Moreover the qualitative advance in weaponry, which is even more significant than the quantitative (which is what SALT agreements cover), brings nearer and nearer the day when the only response for which there will be time is automatic 'launch on warning'. This is the final dehumanisation of war, for computers do not have consciences and can be trusted not to hesitate. But unfortunately they cannot be trusted not to go wrong, and if the track record of the American ones which we know (or partially know) inspires little confidence, the potential reliability of the Russian ones sends shivers down the spine. Even within the present utterly mad system it is desperately important to withdraw from the position of forcing either first strike or launch on warning. Sheer prudential self-interest demands it.

What we urgently need is a defence policy which we could actually *use*. It is not within my technical expertise to propound this: that is why I am interested in the work of the Alternative Defence Commission at Bradford. The Max Planck Institute in Germany has also been putting some of the best minds in Europe to the problem – though both, typically, are under threat of cuts.[10] Already interest has been expressed in army circles, which are the first to see the craziness of the present strategy. And countries like Austria and Sweden, Switzerland and Yugoslavia, who either cannot or will not have nuclear weapons, but who do not want the Soviets rolling across their land any more than anyone else, have been giving far more attention than we have to genuine *defence* policies. Simply competing in chariots, as the prophets would have put it, i.e., in tanks, would be impossible for them, or probably for NATO as a whole. But a large number of dispersed, light precision-guided missiles using the latest heat-homing and laser-beam technologies could inflict unacceptable losses on invading tanks and planes. They would be purely defensive, posing no threats to anyone else. They could not finally stop a determined invader but combined with real training in non-violent and guerrilla resistance, which must already have made the Soviets think twice about another Czechoslovakia or Afghanistan, they would be a powerful shield of freedom for any country not already disintegrating from distorted economic and social priorities aggravated by the arms race.

For this is the real danger. If you fear revolution look within. At the moment we seem to be going the best way to ensure that we are both 'red and dead'. There is no surer recipe for a Communist, or indeed for a Fascist, take-over, or ultimately for a North-South war, than to go on destabilising our society and our world as we are doing. If the Soviets are forced to military intervention in Poland, which they can see would *solve* nothing, it will not be because they are on the march West (they have enough on their hands with their own decaying empire), but because they cannot tolerate a social situation which is dangerously subversive to their system. Such a move would be a sign of weakness rather than strength – and no less perilous for that. But for the West then to renege on arms control would be about the most stupid response possible. Yet it still looks the most likely response.

What should be our response, before it is too late? Surely a massive campaign of conscientisation to bring people to the point of saying 'This is no way to live.' At the moment they go along like sheep (or is it lemmings?) because they believe, to coin a phrase, there is no alternative. They are told that the balance of terror has kept peace, the cold peace, for thirty-five years, and until we have put something else in its place it is dangerous to dismantle it or, like the CND, to undermine it. But meanwhile the arms race goes on escalating and the 'assurance' of mutual destruction looks as uncertain and as crazy as its acronym MAD. It is the new technological 'advances', if that is the right word, which are making the situation inherently unstable. We cannot just go on in the hole we have been in, even if it has hitherto brought relative security. I believe we must resolutely refuse to accept, as Professor Martin put it in his first 1981 Reith Lecture, that 'the best we can do is tidy up the hole and shore up its sides.' That is spiritual, and almost certainly physical, death.

Above all, we must recognise, as the Brandt Report said, that 'more arms do not make mankind safer, only poorer.'[11] And poorer means more destabilised. Look at the food short-

ages in the Soviet Union, the queues in Poland, the rum-
blings in southern Africa and central America, the
unemployed and the rioters on our own streets. This is no
way to go on. Our planet, it has been said, shows the
symptoms of a terminal illness. Yet cancer is hardly the
proper analogy – for our condition is man-made. I heard a
better one the other day used by Dr Rosalie Bertell, that
remarkable, because very unremarkable, nun who as a public
health consultant has shown what a single individual can do
by patient scientific and political slog in bringing home the
effects of so-called 'safe' low-level radiation; she said it is
like living with a drug-addict or alcoholic in the family. The
strain eventually tells on everyone, until one reaches the
point when one cannot cover up or carry on without the
whole home disintegrating. That is the effect of the arms
race on the entire family of man, and particularly, of course
on the poor. If this is what is meant by keeping the peace,
then we must say as strongly as we can 'This is no peace.'

Earlier this year I stood in the extreme north-east corner
of the state of Israel, within striking distance of the Sea of
Galilee. Yet the last thing that would have come to mind
were the lines of the well-known hymn,

> *O sabbath rest by Galilee,*
> *O calm of hills above!*

For this was the notorious Golan Heights, wrested from
Syria by Israel in the six-day war and partly re-occupied by
Syria in the Yom Kippur War, at fearful cost to both sides.
The capital of the Golan is now a ghost town stranded in a
demilitarised zone uneasily policed by the UN force, whose
job is simply to keep the two sides apart. We were told that
the lone Austrian soldier would be glad for a chat with
anyone, but even he was not to be drawn out into the biting
wind. So this was peace-keeping – the best that the human
race can apparently do with all the international resources at
its disposal. Never has the contrast between peace-keeping
and peace-making struck me so forcibly.

I have come to be persuaded that the distinctively Christian
contribution may not perhaps be at the moral level, let alone
the technical. Most of what I have been saying so far could

have been said by anyone, Christian or non-Christian. It has been concerned with the making and keeping of life human, and Christians claim no exclusive wisdom or prerogative in this, though I would hope they would respond to the *humanum* more deeply and broadly and unconditionally as a result of what they have seen in Christ and him crucified. Yet I believe they may have two distinctive – though not again exclusive – things to bring to the present situation, if they are true to the faith and the hope that is in them.

The first concerns what is involved in peace-*making*. The phrase is surprisingly rare even in the New Testament. In fact except in the beatitude 'Blessed are the peace-makers' it occurs only in one other context, where St Paul refers to God in Christ 'making peace by the blood of his cross'.[12] That was the cost of the call to be God's son. And we should remember how the beatitude continues: 'How blest are the peace-makers, God shall call *them* his sons.'[13] When Jesus said to his friends on his last night 'My peace I give to you, not as the world gives do I give you', he passed on this fearful call.[14] For it is the fate of the peace-maker to be crucified, whether in word or in deed, as countless peace-makers of our generation, and not only Christians, have discovered, often at the hands of their own side. No one who is not ready for this need apply for the role.

Second, there is a perspective to the Christian life beyond even this. For the first time for two thousand years we live in a generation where many of the young do not expect to reach middle or old age. In fact according to a BBC opinion poll taken in 1980 some 50 per cent believe the world will see a nuclear war by 1990. If so then my grandson born last year has but a half-chance of reaching the age of ten. But the first Christians too thought that they had but a short time to live, and they did not wring their hands or let it make them depressed or resigned. One of them wrote:[15]

Since the whole universe is to break up in this way, think what sort of people you ought to be. . . . That day will set the heavens ablaze until they fall apart, and will melt the elements in flames. But we have his promise and look forward to new heavens and a new earth, the home of justice.

In fact the world did not end as the early Christians thought. And, pray God, that 50 per cent of the people in our poll will be wrong. Yet that now depends far more on us than it did on them; for we have it within our power to set in motion or to avert the ordeal which is to come upon the whole earth. But staring with clear eyes into the abyss delivered them from moral numbing. They had a hope, and it set them looking and working towards a new world which would be a 'home of justice', a world with its priorities right.

For the Christian, even the total annihilation of this planet is not the end of the world. And the perspective which this gives is vitally important, and vitally important to get right. For it might suggest that the Christian could regard this world as a write-off – and some indeed have drawn this conclusion. Yet, according to the New Testament, reflected classically in the second-century Epistle to Diognetus, the Christian style of life is marked by an extraordinary combination of detachment and concern.[16] The Christian will care less for this world and at the same time care more for it than one who is not. He will not lose his heart to it, but he may well lose his life for it. Though difficult to define, this life style is not I think difficult to recognise when authentically seen, even, or perhaps supremely, in so unpoliticised an example as Mother Teresa. And it manifests itself in that most distinctive conjunction of suffering and joy, of endurance and hope (very different from optimism, which is based on rosy prospects of which there are few around), and even of *hilaritas*.

How is one to come to terms with the fact that unless we in our generation solve the question of nuclear war there will be no other questions? Does one therefore allow oneself to think of nothing else, to become totally obsessed by it? I suggest not. For that is not only liable to become counter-productive ('he can talk of nothing else'). It is a neurotic reaction, making one part of the problem rather than of the solution. Rather it is because I am passionately keen to get on with the hundred and one other things – to write a book on the Fourth Gospel, to enjoy my grandchildren and our

new home in the Yorkshire Dales in this still beautiful world
– that I feel so concerned and committed.

That is the attachment. And the detachment can perhaps
be caught in an answer Sister Rosalie Bertell gave to the
question, 'But aren't you afraid what they can do to you?'
'Why should I be? There's nothing they can take. I haven't
a job. I have no possessions.' Most of us cannot say that
literally. But spiritually there is a freedom from this world
which is the secret of freedom for it. And that is what the
New Testament means by being 'risen with Christ'. It means
walking with a lighter, less earth-bound step even in an
unprecedentedly dark world.

Jonathan Dimbleby

The media and defence: past and future problems

I do not want to put the case in this article for any particular nuclear option, but rather to argue that the media really must begin that sustained and serious debate which has for so long been promised and for so long disgracefully withheld.

Now, some people may wonder why I am complaining. After all, the issue of nuclear war has hardly been out of the headlines for weeks. From President Reagan's gaffes, through to the contradictory statements of his lieutenants, on to his promise to negotiate in earnest, and the fanfares proclaiming the opening of the Geneva talks, the media have been assiduous in their coverage of the nuclear theatre. This rare concern with the subject is a remarkable demonstration of the power of public opinion in a democracy to force reluctant politicians to emerge into the limelight, in the hope of demonstrating that they understand the incomprehensible and have resolved the self-contradictory. There is no dicta-torship, not even that of the proletariat, in which the defence establishment could thus be obliged to leave its bunker in response to the will of the people. But if the principles which sustain democracy are to be nurtured rather than violated, the media – television, radio and newspapers – must no longer be content to echo the response of the defence estab-lishment to the anxieties – and arguments – of what is now known as the Peace Movement.

Of course, the media should report the speeches and de-cisions of those who have their fingers on or near the nuclear button. However, it is an elementary but fundamental pro-position that the role of the media in a free society is to question and analyse prevailing assumptions and attitudes and not merely to regurgitate the conclusions that flow from them for the edification of an uninformed populace. Jour-nalists, that is, should not be town criers or toast masters.

Happily, most of us know it. Most of us for most of the time are unwilling to succumb to the flattery of those in high places who invite journalists to put their ears to the keyhole of the corridors of power to hear the discreet echoes of important whispers – on the implicit understanding, never stated, that a sympathetic interpretation of these great issues would be much appreciated and, who knows, might even lead to a private moment with the Minister where that statesman might permit an indiscretion or two to pass his lips, not for attribution, of course, but so – dear boy – that you may fully understand what is required of us (and you) in the national interest. As I say, it is customary to resist such blandishments. And while we do not expect the crime correspondent to be the first to investigate a case of police corruption, or the City man a financial scandal, we do learn – at least from time to time – about corruption and scandal. And although the lobby correspondent will doubtless preserve the secret that his parliamentary deep throat is a scheming horse-trader of vaulting ambition and no talent, yet every sliver of every split in the two major political parties is thoroughly examined and exhaustively reported.

When I was preparing *The Bomb*, a senior colleague of the ITV company concerned kept asking, 'This is not going to be some kind of unilateralist tract is it, Jonathan?' I said, 'No, it is not' (nor do I believe it was either). His intervention, however, went no further. He was merely offering the knee-jerk 'consensus' warning that I was free to ignore – freer perhaps than some. The problem is that so many adequately honourable executives in television are inadequately informed; they are the first to fall victim to the propaganda by which fundamental but complex dilemmas are so often obscured. It is this – far more than 'censorship' – that stands most persistently in the way of the truth. There is no coherent set of principles – apart from legal constraints – that impose a framework of censorship upon the British media. Censorship exists: but it is generally self-imposed. Most journalists recognise that their freedom of expression is imprisoned by a perimeter fence that is undefined, almost invisible, but may be crossed only at great personal risk to reputation, promotion and even – for persistent transgressors

– to livelihood. This perimeter fence is coterminous with the limits of the consensus established by the normal scope of parliamentary debate.

The starkest and most extreme example of this is the case of British journalism in Northern Ireland – where the fence is made of electrified barbed wire, beyond which is the dangerous minefield where only the brave or the foolhardy dare tread upon the principal assumptions that sustain the British struggle against what is defined – inadequately if understandably – simply as 'the enemy', which is therefore beyond the scope of thoughtful, regular, detailed or controversial analysis.

Now, pressures of this extreme kind do not apply in the matter of defence. Yet, there have been no serious efforts to peer through the propaganda at the fabric of the Western world's nuclear strategy, with the purpose of exploring the dilemmas, contradictions and conflicts with which it is riven. On the other issues of great political moment, we are used to headlines like 'Ted slams Maggie', but have you seen 'Carver slices Nott' or alternatively, 'Nott splices Carver'? Indeed, only those who may have read the correspondence column of *The Times* on 4 November 1981 would even be expected to know to what such a headline might refer. And yet on 4 November Lord Carver, the former Chief of Defence Staff, asserted in public that NATO's strategy for Europe, 'has been incredible and irrational for over twenty years'. And in writing of what NATO is pleased to call 'flexible response' – the core of the strategy of the defence of Western Europe – he stated that 'to initiate nuclear war would not redress or restore the situation; it would be an act of unredeemable folly.' Now since this is – to put it mildly – an unambiguous contribution to the nuclear argument; and since it pertains somewhat directly to no less than the survival of civilisation, one might expect Lord Carver's words to have been of more than passing interest, and therefore to merit some such a headline in one newspaper or another, and perhaps even a mention on radio or television. Yet – unless I missed it – there were no such reports, no such comments.

Since that letter happens to take us to the heart of what is or should be a fundamental controversy, and since I do not subscribe to the conspiracy theory, at least as it applies to journalism in Britain, I find the media's failure puzzling – not least because it is only one example, taken almost at random, from a persistent, almost systematic failure to promote a serious nuclear debate. So why is it?

There is first, of course, the problem of secrecy. Let us admit the requirement to protect national or – in the case of NATO – international security by preserving from public scrutiny that information which may be of dangerous advantage to an adversary. Nevertheless, it hardly needs stating that the Defence Establishment has sedulously protected its empire from inconvenient snoopers. To make matters worse most of the correspondents who are regularly invited to enter those portals tend to favour a somewhat *Boy's Own* approach to their subject, happy to juggle 'relative fire powers' and 'kill ratios', as they assemble for their readers and viewers the technical nuts and bolts of what they evidently accept to be 'necessary murder'. They avoid abstract debate over those strategic doctrines that form the theology of nuclear deterrence. As a result, NATO's strategy and the assumptions upon which it has been built have rarely been put to the test in public. Thus secrecy succours ignorance, begetting indifference.

Let me add that Soviet nuclear strategy has not been put to the test of domestic opinion either. Talking with a Soviet Radio reporter after the Hyde Park rally in 1981, I asked what kind of airtime he had been given back in Russia. He replied, 'three minutes, including E. P. Thompson'. But somehow – as he admitted – Thompson's powerful assault on the Soviet SS-20s had been excluded from his report. Soviet coverage of the Peace Movement in the West is extensive but distorted, wholly ignoring any Western criticism of Kremlin policy. But it does not thereby follow that the Peace Movement is deceiving itself, or the rest of the nation. Although the Eastern bloc systems do not permit the public expression of open opposition, the Soviet elite is not a monolith. There are conflicts within the Soviet establishment; there exist hawks and doves; there is debate and argument, albeit in secret. It is not futile to seek for the adoption of policies in the West that strengthen the peace-mongers in the East.

On the contrary, it is foolish and dangerous to insist that relations between East and West must depend upon a symmetry of communication and information on both sides, and therefore to insist that while asymmetry persists, argument and persuasion in the West is invalid or treacherous. There is misinformation on both sides; there are alternative policies for the West that deserve far more serious attention than most of our media and our establishment are willing – regardless of the Kremlin's response – seriously to consider. Nor, indeed should we entirely disregard the demonstrators in East Germany or Rumania who came on to the streets against the proliferation of nuclear weapons in the European theatre. Are they really to be seen merely as Soviet agents? In *Rumania*? Or are they, by the limited means available to them and within the confines of dissidence from Moscow that their governments are permitted, asserting hopes for the world that are not so far removed from those of the Peace Movement?

As it is, our media is evidently not willing to examine the nature of the Soviet threat; hardly prepared, for instance, to accommodate the proposition that the Kremlin is motivated more by fear than greed.

I find persuasive the view that the Soviet Union is not about to try and grab Western Europe but is more concerned to protect its own empire from the Western 'threat', but even if I am wrong, the assessment deserves serious inspection if our 'free' press is to exercise adequately its responsibilities.

If the media distorts and oversimplifies the purpose of the Soviet Union it has been no less craven in its coverage of the Peace Movement. Twenty years ago it was possible for government, echoed by the media, to dismiss the opposition of our defence dissidents as odd-ball or irrelevant – as a bunch of weirdos, hippies and fellow travellers, cloned with a few confused intellectuals and dissident priests who had managed to misinterpret God's message to man. To express horror of nuclear incineration or to admit to an emotion about the survival of the human family was found embarrassing, if not downright wet. Protected by the media's patronising contempt for this alternative opinion, the defence establishment was left free to accumulate even more nuclear weapons that were ever more sophisticated and which required ever more refined strategies to justify their manufacture; a vicious circle of design, production and deployment in which scientists, technicians, manufacturers and generals clasped each other in that clandestine nuclear embrace which Eisenhower, in high anxiety, called the 'military-industrial complex': a vicious circle that no mere politician could readily understand or felt disposed to penetrate. Indeed, the responsible politicians, dressed up as statesmen for set-piece speeches at the UN and elsewhere, did little more than imprint a populist seal upon a nuclear strategy that had acquired its own momentum, presenting each *fait accompli* over which they had enjoyed virtually no influence as if it were the consequence of careful deliberation in which they had been personally involved at the very highest level. In vain the Zuckermans and the Mountbattens raised their voices in protest, to utter warnings that were smoothly derided by the flinty faced experts in the Pentagon and elsewhere, who had no experience of the war and no nuclear imagination and to whom democracy had entrusted – or rather surrendered – our nuclear future. And the media? Acquiescent or indifferent, as usual, they allowed such warnings to echo in the void beyond the consensus that is enshrined in supine parliaments which still apparently defined the limits of proper public debate.

Thus even two years ago, as you might have expected, NATO's decision – taken like so many others after secret discussion – to deploy cruise and Pershing II missiles in Western Europe was reported with little comment, as a matter of interest principally because two NATO members, Belgium and Holland, where a public debate had been forced upon parliament, had set conditions upon their acceptance of the new missiles on their soil. It would then have seemed inconceivable that the 'modernisation' – and the term was rarely put in quotation marks – of NATO's European armoury might be reversed, or that the issue could become so divisive that reasoned and detached voices would be heard wondering whether the Atlantic Alliance of thirty-five years could survive the strain. Certainly the extraordinary upsurge of public opposition to cruise and Pershing missiles in Europe began despite the prevailing attitude of the media which has generally interpreted the ominous developments of the last two years in terms designed to sustain a hawkish Western attitude towards the Soviet Union. It was an attitude which welcomed a new American president committed to a tough stand against what was called Soviet 'adventurism', which entailed a re-armament programme on an unprecedented scale, that included a nuclear build-up designed to allow Washington to negotiate with Moscow (in return for good behaviour) from what was ominously described as 'a position of strength', which naturally required – for the first time on the soil of Western Europe – the deployment of nuclear missiles that could reach deep into the Soviet Union and which would remain under the sole control of the United States. It is worth noting in passing, that the self-same media which so readily castigated those who described Reagan's approach to world affairs as unrealistic and dangerous now sigh with relief at President Reagan's apparent change of heart, his new maturity and sense of realism.

The groundswell of public opposition that NATO's decision provoked was pretty well ignored by the media, doubtless because it was still hidden beneath the surface that is so assiduously trawled for good stories. Anyway, while the media were still promoting Reagan Mark I, a poll commissioned by the BBC for a radio programme called 'Who's Afraid of the Bomb?' (that had originally been conceived as something of a requiem for CND), revealed the startling statistic that seven out of ten people were more anxious about the proliferation of nuclear weaponry than they were about, for instance, the state of our industrial relations (which in the year of the 'winter of discontent' had been a topic of some moment). Moreover, more than half the population (on the basis of the poll) said that they expected to be engulfed by nuclear war within their lifetime, and most of them were alarmed about the prospect but felt powerless to prevent it. As that deep public feeling began to find its voice, the media – again, I must stress, with honourable exceptions – began anew to echo the politicians in power who thought that they could once more strangle the Peace Movement by dismissing it with the repeated use of that term which connotes the following characteristics: well-meaning, naive, romantic, muddle-headed, emotional, cowardly, unpatriotic, subversive, dangerous – that catch-all condemnation: unilateralist. The evident purpose was to reassure the uncommitted that the minister was right and those who thought otherwise were – well – 'unilateralist'. It failed. It failed because it did not meet the public mood and, no less important, it did not match the evidence. And so, to the dismay of the defence establishment, the fears deepened and, from the point of view of NATO, contaminated more and more of the population. As a result statesmen were obliged to change their tone. Unilateralism was still the code word, but it became possible to detect what Secretary of State Haig might have described in his inimitable fashion as 'a shift in the adjectival emphasis when you parse out the meaning nuance-wise'; i.e., less of the unpatriotic, more of the naive.

The shift continues, although for the most part the presentation of these dreadfully grave issues remains distorted and facile. For a start – to take a simple example to which I will confine my attention – it is not true that you have to be a unilateralist to oppose the deployment of cruise and Pershing missiles on European soil. There is a complex and interwoven set of arguments that can be marshalled in favour of a range of positions between the 'steady as she goes' multilateralist to the 'get rid of them all' enthusiasm of the ultra-unilateralist. Some of the most notable critics of NATO's policy would be outraged to hear themselves described, in even the most minimal sense, as unilateralist. Yet this is rarely reflected in the media.

To my knowledge, there has yet to appear in the British media any full examination of the case for and against cruise and Pershing missiles with the principal arguments laid out carefully and plainly for the intelligent layman to understand. Of course, in our 'free' press, the opposition has not been silenced. The views of Paul Warnke (the SALT II Chief Negotiator) arguing that cruise and Pershing, so far from strengthening NATO, pose a serious threat to the security of Western Europe, once filled a page in the *Guardian*.[1] But his case rested there, never filtering through to a wider audience, while editorials elsewhere continued to offer arthritic homilies about the Soviet threat to sustain a NATO policy whose advocates carefully eschewed serious debate. And what about McGeorge Bundy, Assistant for National Security Affairs to both Kennedy and Johnson? This is what he has written: 'When it is carefully considered, the proposal [to deploy cruise and Pershing] is neither necessary nor desirable for the safety of the alliance.' He goes on, 'the SS-20 [the Soviet weapon that is said by NATO to be the justification for the deployment of cruise and Pershing] did not and does not give the Soviet Union any nuclear capability against Europe alone that it did not have in overflowing measure before a single SS-20 was deployed', and 'on this quite basic point, the simplistic analyses of some nuclear planners, in NATO and elsewhere, have been deeply misleading to their political superiors.' And he goes on:

With a single important exception, there is nothing the 572 new US warheads can do that cannot be done as well by other systems that the United States already has or plans to have. . . . There is indeed one thing some of the new missiles can do that no other weapon can do, but it is something Americans should not want to be able to do.

Citing the fact that Pershing II is designed to reach the Soviet Union – even Moscow itself – within five minutes, he concludes:

It is not for the United States to be the one who first puts the decapitation of the great rival government on a hair trigger. It is deeply in the general interest of all that neither side should pose such threats to the other.

Now this was printed, but not by the British media. It appeared in the *Washington Post*.[2] Nor does it matter for the purposes of this argument whether he is right or wrong – but surely his views (like many other non-unilateralists I could have cited) are of some significance, worthy of some exploration, some analysis, some comment. Instead we are repeatedly and incautiously instructed to rejoice in the fact that Washington has at last been persuaded by Western Europe to open negotiations with Moscow; which is rather like applauding the grand old Duke of York for marching us

down the hill which we had no need to ascend, back to
where we were before.

Nor is it without moment that Professor Michael Howard,
who (and it is meant with no disrespect) is something of a
guru for the defence establishment, has argued, yet again in
the correspondence columns of *The Times*, on 3 November
1981, that 'there [is] no military requirement whatever' for
the theatre nuclear forces. He went on to state that 'there is
no consensus in the European Defence Community, and no
sense among the European peoples as a whole, that the SS-
20s present a threat of a new order of magnitude.' From
which it may be inferred not only that cruise and Pershing
are militarily superfluous but that the defence establishment
is by no means as united on the issue as its public demeanour
might suggest. Now this absence of consensus is precisely
what a vigilant media should have uncovered long ago. Instead our editors are content merely to reveal confusing gusts
of East-West confrontation, reported in isolation, out of
context, from this speech or that – edited highlights almost
without meaning. The failure to explore the political and
military dilemmas of NATO is the more remarkable because
for the first time we are witnessing, under the pressure of
popular opinion, not exactly the break-up of the defence
establishment itself, but, which is of immense significance,
the erosion of its moral and intellectual self-assurance. The
vicious circle is cracking on the circumference. In this tur-
moil it is simply not good enough for the media to gesture
patronisingly in the direction of the opposition by acknow-
ledging that its voice must be heard, but then distorting the
message before going on to reassure us that the angels on
this occasion are yet again those who side with the status
quo, while the unilateralists, albeit unwittingly, are supping
with the devil.

In order to conduct a serious nuclear debate there are
important psychological barriers for the media to overcome.
It takes courage to explore the alternatives to what we may
call 'the NATO perspective'. Now, this is not easy: to pursue
the uncertain path of an argument to an uncertain destination
requires not only courage but resilience and commitment. It
is much simpler, less agonising, to support the status quo in

the comforting belief that 'they' know best and that to contemplate other ways is vaguely disloyal. It is disconcerting
to be brought face to face with ideas that challenge our
established view of the world, that contradict what most of
our peers believe, that challenge the consensus, and verge on
dissidence.

It is even more difficult when dissidents from the other
side become warriors for NATO. The luminaries of the
Peace Movement can play anti-war games with generals and
win, despite the ridicule and contempt that is heaped upon
them. But how does an honest media handle the courageous
Soviet scientist Vladimir Bukovsky who spent years inside
a psychiatric hospital, where he endured unspeakable suffering, merely for the crime of dissidence. Now that he is a free
man in Western exile, this distinguished scientist argues with
passion that the Soviet Union is indeed bent on world domination and that the CND, wittingly or not, is aiding and
abetting that purpose. Since his views were given great
prominence in *The Times*,[3] the Peace Movement is obliged
to insist that this remarkable man's understanding of the war
game is too limited to deserve our close attention. Only the
callow could enjoy thus dismissing a brave and brilliant man.
The Peace Movement has no choice; and the media's role
should be to adjudicate between them, not to use one dissident to discredit another.

If we are to reach towards an understanding of the nuclear
crisis – and it is by no means too late – the media must
overcome the habit of deference to the establishment. They
must start by admitting that the term 'unilateralist' is now
so burdened by invective that it has ceased to have any useful
meaning for the purpose of serious argument. So, let it be
discarded, at least by honourable politicians and honourable
editors, except to describe that small section of the opposition which would campaign for wholesale nuclear disarmament in every country of NATO not excluding the United
States, whether or not there is any Soviet response to such
unilateral action.

If the media were to kick the 'unilateralist' habit, they
might wake up with a clearer head in the morning; might
see the point in diverting some of their formidable forensic

talent from the intimate contemplation of domestic affairs
– whether royal marriage or political divorce – to the inves-
tigation of the true purpose and uncertain prospects of the
disarmament talks in Geneva. It had been reported – end-
lessly and obediently – that NATO hopes to achieve the
so-called zero option. Belatedly it has also been suggested
that the zero option is unattainable: that it was proposed by
anxious European members of NATO hoping to defuse the
Peace Movement, in the full knowledge that it would be an
impossible negotiating position to sustain. But what has been
almost ignored by the British media is the revelation, reported on 28 October 1981 by the *New York Times* that:

*Many European officials [in NATO] would be disappointed if Moscow
accepted the zero option approach. . . . The adoption of the zero option
at the beginning of the coming talks is a necessary public relations move.
They hoped it would link in the minds of their uneasy constituents the
Long-range US nuclear tipped missiles with the Russian SS-20s.*

And the report added that the zero option – far from being
a brave new step for mankind – was originally rejected by
the Carter Administration on the grounds that 'the Soviet
Union would not consider the Allies serious in wanting some
arms limitation . . . if it were adopted.'

NATO propaganda can only triumph if those uneasy constituents to which the *New York Times* referred remain in the
dark. And, with the exception of a belated nudge and wink
here and there, that is precisely what has happened. Wittingly
or not – and regardless of whether the zero option turns out
to be a good negotiating tactic or not – the British media
have done for NATO what Saatchi and Saatchi did for the
Tories in 1979.

I reach no simple conclusion. We cannot merely say that
because the media are committed to NATO, they disdain
alternative argument. Conspiracy theorists inhabit a fantasy
world: Government does not impose a point of view upon
the hierarchies of the BBC and ITV which is then transmitted
by secret edict to programme makers for transmission to the
nation; nor is the national press (however imprisoned by the
market place that nourishes their proprietors) under orders
to impose their distortions upon us. The problem originates

with the political consensus that is still permitted to define the proper limits of public debate. Thus for twenty years until the start of this decade, nuclear weapons were judged to be virtually irrelevant to the business of parliament. Politicians did not discuss nuclear strategy; they were, and generally are, ignorant about the complexities of NATO policy; the media, defining its purpose as a forum for debate about matters of 'public concern' remained supine; and the public was left to peer through the glass darkly.

If the media were now to display a little more zeal in pursuit of nuclear truths they could transform our understanding not only of the Geneva talks, but of their relationship to other, no less urgent issues: the controversy about flexible response; the doctrine of limited nuclear war; the concept of 'balance' in a world of nuclear overkill; the prospect of another dangerous spiral in the arms race; the risk of an accidental holocaust that begins ludicrously from miscalculation or misunderstanding; and, finally, to that gravest of all, the question of whether the prevailing strategies are protecting the peace or driving us towards the abyss. It is surely not too much to insist that commonsense requires the debate to begin in earnest without delay.

E. P. Thompson

A mid–Atlantic moderate

Editors' Note

The 1981 BBC Reith lectures – 'The Two-Edged Sword' – were concerned with nuclear strategy and the search for security. They were broadcast by Professor Laurence Martin, Vice-Chancellor of the University of Newcastle upon Tyne in November and December. Over the same period the Alternative Reith lectures were delivered at the University of Newcastle upon Tyne. The Alternative Reith lectures were not conceived as a reply to, or an anticipation of, Professor Martin's lectures; however they provide numerous occasions for comparison. We pause here to note briefly the extent to which the debate has been joined by the parallel events.

Professor Martin's six lectures were entitled: 'If you knows of a better 'ole . . .', 'Plausibility and Horror', 'Shadow over Europe', 'Conflicts in the Third World', 'Not for the Sake of their Blue Eyes' and 'Who's Moving the Goal Post?'. The titles are indicative of a style which must leave some of Professor Martin's listeners and readers unsure of his meaning. The second of his lectures was primarily concerned with doctrines of strategic nuclear deterrence, the third with the military balance in Europe. The fourth lecture included discussion of the prospects for nuclear non-proliferation and consideration of Western interests within the Third World; the conflicts in the Third World of most concern to Professor Martin were those between the West and the Soviet Union. The fifth lecture concerned arms control – sharply distinguished from disarmament and conceived as an integral part of defence and security. The final lecture presented a vision of absolute military security as an unattainable goal; but it also included a discussion of Britain's strategic role and its last few minutes were devoted 'to the matter of public opinion.'

Professor Martin's lectures appeared in the Listener *and are published by Weidenfeld & Nicolson. A detailed comparison with the preceding lectures in this volume is therefore possible. Compare for example: Martin's policy for Britain with Galtung's conceptions of security; Martin's view of the relevance of moral considerations with that of John Robinson; the clearly incompatible evaluations of the military balance by Martin and Kaldor; Martin's references to the significance of*

*technological development with Pentz's detailed discussion of the
implications of development in missile technology; and the discussions by
Martin and Dimbleby of public debate and opinion.*

*Professor Martin's first lecture was a general introduction. It began by
asserting 'the supreme importance of averting an all-out nuclear war',
but it ended by stating what many will consider to be his principal
conclusion 'after some years of surveying the no-man's-land of strategic
theory, I have yet to find a better hole than our present balance of
power.' All the contributors to this volume would make the assertion
wholeheartedly their own but would vigorously reject the conclusion.*

Professor Laurence Martin is not a pushy kind of fellow. He
has crept up upon the British public by stealth. His publications are slender, but every paper has been placed judiciously and under prestigious auspices. He is 'an accepted
figure in military circles' (we have been told in a *Times*
profile), and has lectured to 140 NATO admirals, all in full
uniform, in Norfolk, Virginia, drawing applause at the end.
If the British public had not heard of him until last month
it is because he is so self-effacing, and has been so busy
interpreting our wishes over there in (the *Guardian*'s profile
tells us) the 'world of strategic thinkers and generals and
Pentagon heavies'.

Professor Martin is the soul of modesty. He would not
wish us to be in too much awe of him as a heavy. Although
he has come before us, on six occasions, as the BBC's Reith
lecturer, he is aware that there is little that he could do for
us in such a limited time: 'I have devoted some of the brief
time available to attacking some of the sacred cows of the
less inhibited disarmers,' he noted in his final lecture. It
seems clear that, if pushed a little, he might be willing to
spare the time to attack them more.

But if he has attacked disarmers, he has the candour to
add that he has done so 'not out of contempt but out of a
due appreciation of their influence and importance'. It is
reassuring to learn that one has not provoked the contempt
of so distinguished and so authoritative a mind. Professor
Martin also believes in fair play; he 'cannot regret free discussion'. That is reassuring also; although a free discussion
in which we are visited in our homes on six occasions with-

out a right of reply might seem to be a little deficient in that quality of which he is so eloquent an advocate: 'balance'.

It was, without doubt, the ungraciousness of the BBC, in limiting Professor Martin to such a brief time, which prevented him from explaining *everything* to us. He simply was not afforded space to analyse the evidence, nor to deploy new facts. Time and again he was forced to fall back upon mere assertion. This is, perhaps, why even his most brilliant polemics fell short of conviction. Thus, in his first lecture, he smartly took out three of the sacred cows of disarmers in the space of three minutes. Observe his mode of attack.

The first cow was identified as the 'so-called "military-industrial complex" the alleged conspiracy of soldiers and armament manufacturers' who exaggerate the dangers of the antagonist in order to promote their 'own political and economic interests'. Observe the marksmanship of 'so-called' and of 'alleged conspiracy'. That cow is desperately wounded by ridicule before even a shot has been fired. What moderate and balanced mind could possibly suppose that soldiers or arms manufacturers could conspire or have interests of their own? Not only is the 'military-industrial complex' laughed off the scene, but in the same moment General Eisenhower, Lord Zuckerman and a host of researchers are convicted of idiocy.

But a *coup de grace* is needed for this suffering cow. This is provided by reference to 'a recent, careful, statistical study of the subject', coming from Harvard, according to which tests for 'the presence of arms competition or arms racing' have proved negative. This is a finding of 'behavioural science'. It has been put in at one end of a computer and it has come out at the other end. It must be true. Brilliant as this attack is, Professor Martin overlooked that he was faced here, not by one sacred cow, but by two. Hence his bullet went harmlessly in between them both. For the notion of a military-industrial complex, with its own inherent thrust and interests, and the metaphor of an arms race, whose thrust is derived from competition with the arms of an antagonist, are different and distinct.

Some recent studies have called in question the 'action-reaction' model, by which the upward growth in nuclear

arms is the direct outcome of competition between the ar-
mourers of the two superpowers – that is, a 'race' in its usual
sense. Attention has been redirected to inertial pressures on
both sides – the long waves of R & D (research and development), 'technology creep', the imperatives of the 'alchemists' in the laboratories – which drive arms innovations
forward independently of any direct competition. (As a case
in point, both the SS-20 and the cruise missile were developed independently of the other: it was never a case that one
was a 'response' to the other, however convenient it may
have been in subsequent propaganda to propose them as an
equation.) And I would myself add to this the ideological
drive of 'deterrence theory' itself, which, by continuously
proposing worst-case scenarios as to possible developments
on the other side, engenders new developments on its own
side – and brings forward the worst-case scenario also.

The outcome of all this looks, in commonsense, like a
'race', but the competition between antagonists is indirect,
and the mediations are so complex that they will evade
Harvard's computer. This sacred cow – *both* cows – may
safely graze in the lush pastures of the world's armaments a
little longer. But surely the *next* sacred cow is dead and ready
for dinner? Disarmers are given to rabbiting on about the
rising defence budget in the United States. Yet Professor
Martin is able to show that the military share of the federal
budget *fell* from 49 per cent in 1960 to 23 per cent in 1981,
and President Reagan is proposing only to put that up to 24
per cent in 1981. What a fuss and bother about 1 per cent,
when in the long run the figures have been halved! That
bullet grazes the poor old cow: indeed, it may draw blood.
Nuclear weapons may be hideously costly in their threat to
life but they are not the most costly items in fiscal terms.
Conventional weapons or launching platforms – aircraft carriers, submarines, tanks, bombers – are the major tax-eaters.
An upwards growth in nuclear arms can coexist with a
downward drift in defence budgets.

Yet Professor Martin's aim was not as steady as might be
supposed. He was too eager to make a showy killing. For
a critical change in the procedures of US federal budget
accounting took place between 1965 and 1966. Before that

time the US Administration presented to Congress an 'administrative budget', of direct appropriations from the Treasury, which did not include 'trust funds' – i.e. federal pensions and social security payments, some highway funds, and other moneys separately levied and paid out on the basis of recurrent authorising legislation. But from 1966 these trust funds were included in one overall, greatly-enlarged, federal budget: so that what had appeared before as 40 per cent for defence, re-appeared as 22 per cent of the newly enlarged overall budget. It is the sort of magician's trick for which statistics, in agile hands, are a ready wand.

The Reith lecturer will of course have been aware of this qualification (and it is a large one), and no doubt he would have explained it if the BBC had allowed him time. Meanwhile, that sacred cow may bellow, but she will continue to graze. I am myself a duffer at figures; but if the BBC shares Professor Martin's own enthusiasm for 'free discussion', might it not invite an acknowledged expert, such as Dr Frank Barnaby of Stockholm International Peace Research Institute to comment on the matter?

The third sacred cow taken out is a notion of George Kennan's that 'it has been we Americans, who, at almost every step of the road, have taken the lead in the development of this sort of weaponry'. This, Professor Martin observes sternly, 'is at best a half truth and the half that is true is not patently disgraceful.' Professor Martin does not tell us why Kennan's statement 'is at best a half truth'. What is half untrue about it? And if it is half untrue, why does Martin then himself offer it to us, in his third lecture, as his own unqualified wisdom, when he refers to 'the traditional pattern in which each new technical sophistication has usually appeared first on the Western side?' The notion that technical innovation might be 'disgraceful' is Martin's and not Kennan's. Kennan had simply observed that the United States had led in every major innovation (from the first atomic bomb to thermo-nuclear weapons to MIRVs to cruise missiles), and had been pacemaker in what is now an insanely dangerous process.

But Professor Martin has already swivelled his rifle to take out Admiral Gene La Rocque, who is accused of giving aid and comfort to this same sacred cow. The admiral's offence is to have invited Martin to a conference in Groeningen last May on 'Nuclear War in Europe', with an accompanying letter deploring the new generation of nuclear weapons (which include cruise missiles and Pershing II) as 'more precise and more devastating'. 'Students of the subject' avers Professor Martin, with the assumption of authority which befits a former Professor of War Studies (but not, it seems, a retired admiral), 'will see an element of internal contradiction here: at least it all depends on what you don't want to devastate.' More precise weapons will destroy their targets with more accuracy, and there will be less devastation overall.

'A hit! A palpable hit!' And why is that sacred cow now bellowing and rolling on the ground? Professor Martin would have found out if he had been able to attend the admiral's conference in Groeningen (I do not recall seeing him there) or had read the admiral's own paper. For more accurate weapons can be more dangerous (if not necessarily more devastating) because they may encourage fantasies of the first strike at the opponent's silos (the Pershing II), or may be seen as instruments for nuclear war-fighting in more 'limited' or flexible ways. The old block-busting or city-burning theory of deterrence (MAD) fragments into a dozen scenarios of war-fighting at intermediate levels.

Admiral La Rocque (whose Center for Defense Information in Washington is well informed) considers that the new, and more precise, weapons would make more probable the devastation of the 'theatre' of Europe. In his third lecture, Professor Martin employed the device of caricature to scoff the notion aside: 'Some unilateralists, ably supported by several Soviet research institutes, suggest a positive American eagerness for a limited nuclear war confined to Europe.' Two minutes later, when his argument had taken a different turn, he referred – in an explanatory aside – to 'NATO's old plan of escalating to the theatre level, perhaps involving Soviet territory'. This sacred cow appears to be undeterred; but Professor Martin has suffered a self-inflicted wound.

The lectures went on and on. Martin was folksy and grave by turns. But since the BBC had allowed him so little time, he could spare little of it for facts and even less for arguments. He was reduced, of necessity, to presenting his prejudices and asserting his assertions.

If a lecturer has no original arguments to deploy, and is reduced to mere assertion, then the problem becomes, how can *this* lecturer's assertions appear to be more wise, more authoritative, more judicious than any other's? The critic should attend less to the commonplaces that the lecturer uttered than to the strategy of his delivery. This also was judiciously commonplace, but it deserves to be noted. I have marked my copy of the lectures with a series of 'yes-words' and of 'no-words' which are made to do the work which evidence or argument should have done. The 'boo-words' are what might be expected of a Defence Minister – let us say John Nott – although not, perhaps, of a Reith Lecturer. In the first lecture, disarmers are 'utopian' their attitudes made up of 'intellectual confusion, half-truths and downright error'; they are motivated by 'unreflective anti-militarism or gratuitous denigration of ourselves and our allies'; their impulses are 'dangerous', in some 'naive', in others 'disingenuous'.

In subsequent lectures, such boo-words accumulate, and are compounded with a general pro-Soviet sneer. Opposition to cruise and Pershing missiles ('the Soviet campaign against the NATO decision') is presented as a Soviet intervention in 'the domestic European political debate'. The Soviet Union is given to 'intensive exploitation of well-meaning disarmament lobbies in the West'. Since the motives of these lobbies are suspect, and their intellectual equipment is derisory, their arguments clearly cannot trespass upon the brief time of our distinguished lecturer any further.

The yes-words are more numerous. They suggest academic retirement, prolonged and rigorous study, measured judgment. The arguments of opponents are always 'flawed'; his own assertions are the fruit of 'serious studies'. Asserting that 'the balance of power remains the best guiding principle for strategic policy', he adduces no new argument but falls back upon his own immense authority: 'I can only plead that after many years in strategic studies I have come to the conclusion that . . . ' For all his great modesty, Professor

Martin allows us to know that he has been, over the years, privileged with the confidences of the Great. He introduces the names of his friends unobtrusively, without fuss: 'as Mr Dean Acheson once said to me'; or thus: 'My friend, Albert Wohlstetter, the American strategist, the father of the phrase "the delicate balance of terror" . . . .' Professor Martin's privilege is, deftly, for a passing moment, conferred upon his auditors. How privileged we are also to be listening to an Authority who can number among his friends the father of so perspicacious and so illuminating a phrase!

It is Professor Martin's strategy also to claim always for his judgment less than his listeners would be ready to concede. His judgments (except where disarmers are concerned) are never strident. They are tentative. Sometimes, on questions to which the rabble outside the studio has already snatched at 'easy and popular' remedies, the professor's own decision is refused. If he must come down on one side rather than the other, it is always with reluctance: 'after some years of surveying the no-man's-land of strategic theory, I have yet to find a better hole than our present balance of power'. Even in the moment of decision, he grimaces at the loud absolutes on every side of him: 'I do not rate myself very highly as a moralist,' he avers; or, again, 'it would be presumptious and foolhardy for me to prescribe solutions.' 'In a climate where everybody seems to be pushing some cheap or easy remedy a note of caution may not come amiss.' Even on the matter of whether to purchase Trident he turns aside with reticence: 'I am not fully qualified to judge.'

How admirable this modesty, and how judicious these repeated evasions of open judgments! And if so high an Authority as Professor Martin, with his long and arduous years in strategic studies, confesses that it would be 'presumptious' in him to suggest solutions, how much more incapable we, his unlettered listeners, must be! How brash it is for CND to mill around the streets in its 'easy and popular' way!

Professor Martin's strategy is to put two old tricks together: the arched eyebrow of the academic, raised in disdain and rigour, and the inside know-how of the expert, privy to the confidences of the establishment. He has listened all these years to the dramas of the Great, like Polonius behind the arras. And he chooses just those terms which Polonius, if he had been elevated to a Chair of War Studies instead of being brutally cut short by the blade of a confused disarmer, would have used to decorate his inaugural lecture: 'symmetry', 'appropriateness', 'credible', 'legitimacy', 'modest but intensely practical approaches'. He wishes it to be supposed that he is offering nothing in the least unusual: 'I must confess at the outset that I, at least, have no such complete assurance about the prescriptions that are, on balance, the best I can discover.' He wishes to be taken as just one other in the long line of Reith lecturers: the bland leading the bland. The Reith lecturer, is an *ad hominem* appointment. 'They', or someone up there, decide who is an 'expert' and confer this distinction upon their choice. It is inevitable that we should examine these credentials in our turn, and submit the incumbent to our own *ad hominem* scrutiny.

Yet I cannot be content with a notion of Laurence Martin as Professor Polonius or Professor Pangloss. There is something else to him than that. For his strategy of lecturing was too evident: it was a device, not only for imposing his opinions upon the audience, but also for concealing their true character. There is something more to Professor Martin than 'realism' and 'moderation'.

He has, after all, climbed upwards inexorably, yet it would seem from the newspaper profiles that he has found advancement always by stealth, on an inside track, hidden from public view. His biographers say something about the positions he has held, but little to indicate any intellectual achievement. He has acquired the hubris of the academic, but without acquitting himself in any recognised academic discipline. Indeed, although he is a leading practitioner of strategic studies he 'freely expresses doubts' (*The Times* informs us) 'about whether it should be an academic discipline at all.'

These doubts are well-founded. Strategic studies, if they are not admixed with a reputable discipline – of the economist, the political theorist, or the historian – are a non-discipline. They are the apologetics of military power. They commence with militarist assumptions – as to the virtues of 'deterrence' and the 'balance of terror' – and after long and tedious years of consultancies and conferences around the globe, the very same assumptions are recycled with authority as Reith lectures. The only change is that the 'balance' which must now be maintained is at a higher and more sophisticated level.

Professor Martin is a new kind of intellectual creature. He has prospered as a courtier to the nuclear weapons-systems and their defence establishments. A courtier to them, he is also a courier to us – it is his business to convey to us their imperatives: 'If you speak to the technicians at the nuclear laboratories, you learn that it is not as simple as it looks. The case for Trident appears in a stronger light when you talk to the experts.' He has been employed (he has told the *Guardian*) as a courier on even nicer and more secret matters. It was through him that the Pentagon sent a message to 'the Brits' that it would facilitate the Chevaline modernisation pro-gramme to the Polaris warhead. The 'Brits' who were then informed did not include the British public, nor even the British Cabinet. A courtier, like a courtesan, must know the value of privacy.

Martin's biographers give little away. He went up to Cam-bridge in 1945, when the Second World War had just ended. He did some service in the peacetime RAF. He went on to Yale, to MIT, was a consultant at the NATO defence college and to the Los Alamos weapons laboratories. At Yale he ran a radio show called 'Religion at the Newsdesk', but without unseemly fervour: 'I go to church occasionally. I am not an unreligious man.' He is a great conference-goer, consorting with Dr Kissinger and Caspar Weinberger at Williamsburg, or in the more secret events of the European-American In-stitute for Security Studies ('he hints at the institute's value in keeping Turkey loyal to NATO'). And all of this, which might weigh heavily on some, he has taken lightly, in the best tradition of the English intellectual dilettante. The vice-chancellorship of Newcastle University, which he was gracious enough to accept in 1978, 'he regards in some ways as his first real job'. Lesser men might have supposed that his previous post, as Professor of War Studies at King's

College, London, was a 'real job'. There have been wars enough to study.

He is a new kind of mid-Atlantic creature, whose formative intellectual experiences must have been laid down in that traumatic mid-Atlantic moment, the genesis of the Cold War. His biographers provide only one clue to this formation. Laurence Martin went up to Cambridge in 1945, at the age of seventeen, 'and all his contemporaries were 35 with the Military Cross.' It gave him, he concedes, 'a certain respect for the military'. But something here has been misremembered, and has been skewed into myth. Some of Martin's contemporaries at Cambridge then (of whom I was one) had returned from the services or from other kinds of 'war work': few of them were thirty-five, fewer had the Military Cross, a good number of them were women, and if we shared anything in common it was disrespect for the military and delight at shedding that transient disguise.

Martin's misrecognition of the situation took my mind back to Christopher Isherwood's *Lions and Shadows* – an autobiography of a youth at Cambridge immediately after the First World War:

Like most of my generation I was obsessed by a complex of terrors and longings connected with the idea 'War'. 'War', in this purely neurotic sense, meant The Test. The Test of your courage, of your maturity, of your sexual prowess: 'Are you really a Man?'

How abrupt the mutations of generations, the shifts in cultural cohorts may be! As my 'generation' was just shaking 'War' off itself, as a dog shakes water off its coat, Martin's generation (some four or five years our juniors) was obsessed by the war they had just missed: 'The Test'. Can this obsession have carried him through all these years, all that transatlantic conferring, to the Chair of War Studies and, at last, to the imperial purple of Reith?

Professor Martin has proposed a problem to his own vaulting ambition. There is scarcely anywhere where he can now go, after these distinguished lectures, save into the House of Lords. If I might offer him a small service, I would propose to him a title, appropriate to the courtier of deterrence: Lord Prufrock of Los Alamos:

> . . . *an attendant lord, one that will do*
> *To swell a progress, start a scene or two,*
> *Advise the prince; no doubt, an easy tool,*
> *Deferential, glad to be of use,*
> *Politic, cautious, and meticulous;*
> *Full of high sentence, but a bit obtuse;*
> *At times, indeed almost ridiculous –*
> *Almost, at times, the Fool.*

I propose the title. But now I must take it back. For if we
allow him this, then he has succeeded in his imposture. It
was his strategy to come forward thus; to pretend to offer
a courtier's homiletics; to confirm the bigoted in the good
repute of their bigotry; to reassure the anxious with plati-
tudes; and to leave his opponents with nothing to throw
back save grimaces and names – 'Yah! Prufrock, Pangloss,
Polonius!' The strategy was to come before us as a 'moderate', and make all other views appear as utopian or extreme.

Yet it is Professor Martin who is an extremist. He
advocates some of the most extreme views which it is possible for anyone in our time to hold. He approves of every
deadly weapons-systems which now exists, and he approves
of their continuing innovation. As I run through these lectures and separate the true *import* from its several disguises
I find these judgments. The Polaris submarine is 'a valuable
contribution to several forms of strategic stability.' General
disarmament is undesirable, and would be impossible to
verify. The introduction of cruise and Pershing II missiles
may not be 'essential', but may well be prudent as part of
the 'refurbishment' of 'the whole western nuclear arsenal.'
NATO must continue to reserve to itself the right of first
nuclear use. Nuclear proliferation may be good or bad: a
Libyan bomb would be 'a *terrifying* thought', but an Israeli
one may be a comforting one: 'nevertheless . . . I think the
burden of proof is on anyone who wants to encourage a new
power to join the nuclear ranks.' The arms trade is 'much
denigrated', since it may play 'an essential role in curbing
proliferation' (the superpowers can buy the Third World off
with tanks and bombers instead). A rapid deployment force
(it is implied, in lecture four) is urgent and desirable, and
European nations – in particular Britain and France – should

make more contribution outside Europe. A complete test ban would be bad. Arms control may be permitted, in certain conditions, but it is undesirable to let it be supposed that it can result in *dis*armament. Although 'not fully qualified to judge' the merits of Trident, Professor Martin is in favour of it.

If we do not conclude that these views, taken together, are nihilist and extremist, then we must conclude that the course of civilisation is already run. This is, perhaps, Professor Martin's own conclusion – and the assumption from which he started out.

The first line of lecture one is this: 'Armed force is the ultimate tool of political conflict.' The sentence is intended to echo Clausewitz: but we have come a long way from that old philosopher. War may be the continuation of politics by other means, but the means are *other* than the means of politics. To suggest that armed force is 'the ultimate tool' of politics is to suggest that it is normal, or at least inevitable. Murder may be the continuation of a marital dispute by other means, but we might hesitate before we concluded that murder is 'the ultimate tool' of marital relations. It is the business of civilisation to refuse the means of war just as we refuse the means of murder. Martin, who has other business, regards warfare as normal and peace 'as a kind of suspended war'.

I find these extremist views objectionable. I find it objectionable to refer to the Soviet Union as 'the enemy'. And I find even more objectionable (and disturbing as I write these lines) some views propounded (with moderation) in lecture three. The Polish crisis, Martin argues, 'is dangerous for NATO as well as the Warsaw Pact.' And why is this? The Poles have been immoderate, they have upset stability. Professor Martin is concerned, of course, only with 'strategic implications.' 'It is not my place', he reassures us, 'to explore political possibilities.' But in an impartial *strategic* view it can be seen that 'previous episodes – Hungary, Czechoslovakia, Afghanistan' did nothing to the strategic balance but good. They made NATO 'more lively in its military preparations'. There were more conferences to give papers to, more consulting to do at Los Alamos.

But, gracious heavens, the danger of this episode is that the Poles might *succeed*! And this would encourage 'neutralists and unilateralists' in the West to roll back United States military power as well. This could erode 'European contributions to NATO' and this conjoint prospect, of the Cold War actually *receding* in both halves of Europe, Martin 'would find highly alarming'. No doubt he finds the latest news from Poland to be reassuring. The Cold War will go on. NATO will become 'more lively' once again. As my own vision of the astonishing opportunities of this year, 1981, when we might have begun to put Europe back together, begins to close, Martin's perspectives open once again.

And yet, in this moment of closure and of opening, the terrifying configurations of Professor Martin's form of extremism are suddenly apparent. For he is not, after all, concerned with a discipline within its own compartment: a discrete aspect of human life – strategic studies. He is claiming the *whole* of life. For we glimpse at last that 'the strategic balance' is an on-going social and economic system in itself, to which all other aspects of our lives are now subordinate. Like some gigantic, expanding ectoplasm 'the strategic balance' of nuclear weaponry hangs above us, sucking up everything – our taxes, our hopes, the last outposts of Gaelic culture, the aspirations of the Polish or Greek peoples – into itself. We may do no more than creep (with moderation) beneath it, serving its voracious appetite, keeping The System adjusted. Eventually, we know, it will suck in the eco-sphere itself.

And now at last I can see who Professor Martin is. He is an Alien, descended from that alienated ectoplasmic world, to instruct us in our duties to The System. The Reith lectures were Close Encounters of the Fourth Kind. If we are dutiful, moderate and obedient, we may expect Close Encounters of a Fifth Kind. They will be the last.

Notes

Introduction

1 For a good, brief review of these problems since 1975 see the appropriate sections in the annual *Strategic Survey*, London, International Institute for Strategic Studies, 1975–81.

2 Theatre nuclear forces are a somewhat ambiguous category, since strategic weapons (targeted on the opponent's homeland) can always be re-targeted to hit the battlefield (the actual theatre of fighting). Normally, however, TNFs include missiles launched from submarines, ground-launched missiles with ranges from 3,000 miles down to less then 100 miles, nuclear capable aircraft, and artillery firing nuclear shells.

3 See Simon Lunn, 'Cruise Missiles and Prospects for Arms Control', *Armament and Disarmament Information Unit (ADIU) Report*, University of Sussex, vol. 3, no. 5, Sept./Oct. 1981, pp. 1–5.

4 *Ibid.*, Richard Burt, Director of the Bureau of Political and Military Affairs.

5 On 4 November 1981, United States Secretary of State Haig spoke of NATO plans to explode a 'demonstration' nuclear weapon. This was denied by the Secretary for Defense, Caspar Weinberger, the following day. President Reagan had already spoken of the possibility of a tactical nuclear war in Europe that would exclude a superpower nuclear exchange. This too was denied in clarifications from the Defense Department.

During 1981 the Defense Department admitted to thirty-two nuclear accidents over recent years, mainly concerned with crashes of nuclear bombers. Since 1980 there have also been incidents of false nuclear alerts, a nuclear submarine collision with a cargo ship, and an explosion inside a missile silo which destroyed the missile and threw the warhead 200 feet into the air.

6 For concise reviews of the politics behind such slogans see the annual volumes of *The World Today*. For American views of

the state of the Alliance see in particular, Theodore Draper, 'The Western Misalliance', and Simon Serfaty, 'The United States and Europe', in *The Washington Quarterly*, vol. 4, no. 1, 1981. For a critical European history see, Alfred Grosser, *The Western Alliance*, London, Macmillan, 1980.

7   For a discussion of this decision see, Morton Halperin, *Contemporary Military Strategy*, London, Faber, 1972. On the general problem of limited nuclear war the best text is his *Limited War in the Nuclear Age*, New York, Wiley, 1963.

8   Gregory Treverton, *Nuclear Weapons in Europe*, Adelphi Paper 168, London, International Institute of Strategic Studies, 1981.

9   The first Special Session was held in May–June 1978. The Second Special Session is planned for June–July 1982. The Committee on Disarmament in Geneva has just completed a three year report for submission to the Second Special Session. The CD is a new manifestation, since 1978, of the Conference Committee on Disarmament (CCD) which previously sat in Geneva.

10 *North – South: A Programme for Survival*, London, Pan Books, 1980, ch. 7.

11 *The Times*, 24 April 1980.

12 *Sanity*, no. 5, Oct./Nov. 1981, p. 31.

13 John Cox, *Overkill*, London, Pelican Books, 1981.

14 *The Times*, 14 November 1980.

15 *The Times*, 16 November 1981.

16 *The Times*, 17 November 1981.

17 *Sanity*, no. 6, Dec./Jan. 1981, p. 7.

18 *The Times*, 23 June 1980. The Ecology Party has also supported CND, adopting unilateralism as party policy in 1976 at its first annual conference.

19 *The Times*, 11 September 1981.

20 *The Times*, 23 October 1981.

21 *The Times*, 26 May 1981.

22 *The Times*, 9 June 1981.

23 *The Times*, 6 October 1981.

24 *The Times*, 25 November 1980.

25 *The Times*, 17 September 1981.

26 For further information on these events see, *The Catholic Herald*, 28 August 1981; 3 July 1981; *Church Times*, 12 June 1981; 20 November 1981; *The Times*, 12 September 1981.

27 *Baptist Times*, 18 June 1981.

28 *Financial Times*, 26 October 1981.

29 *Sunday Times*, 26 October 1980.

30 Figures taken from various reports in *Sanity* of the different demonstrations.

31 *New Statesman*, 5 December 1980.

32 *The Times*, 31 August 1981.

33 *Sanity*, no. 6, Dec./Jan. 1981, p. 25.

34 *The Times*, 12 October 1981.

35 David Greenwood and Peter Hennessey 'Defence Choices for the Eighties' (series of articles) *The Times*, 27–30 October 1981. See also David Greenwood, 'Reshaping Britain's Defences', *Aberdeen Studies in Defence Economics*, no. 19, September 1981.

36 *ADIU Report*, vol. 3 no. 3 May/June 1981.

37 The Nott review appeared as, *The United Kingdom Defence Programme: The Way Forward* CMND 8288, London, HMSO, 1981. For comments on its reception see, Greenwood and Hennessey, *op. cit.*

38 Fourth Report from the Defence Committee 1980–1, *Strategic Nuclear Weapons Policy*, HC 36, London, HMSO, 1981.

39 *The Times*, 5 October 1981.

40 *Hansard*, 1980–1, 10 November 1981, column 411.

41 For details of the Marplan Poll see the *Guardian* 22 April 1981.

42 *Statement on the Defence Estimates 1981*, vol. 1, CMND 8212–1, London, HMSO, 1981.

43 *The Times*, 20 May 1981.

44 *The Times*, 12 October 1981.

45 *The Times* 14 November 1981.

46 *Financial Times*, 24 October 1981.

47 *Daily Telegraph*, 9 September 1981.

48 *The Times*, 28 October 1981.

49 *Soviet Military Power*, published 29 October 1981, United States Department of Defense. Available from the United States Embassy.

50 *Hansard*, 1980–1, 19 November 1981, column 417.

51 *Hansard*, 1980–1, 19 May 1981, column 169.

52 *The Times*, 28 October 1981.

53 *Statement on the Defence Estimates 1981*, vol. 1, CMND 8212–1, London, HMSO 1981, p. 13.

54 *Hansard*, 1980–1, 5 November 1981, column 120.

55 *Hansard*, 1980–1, 19 May 1981, column 168.

56 *Hansard*, 1980–1, 5 November 1981, column 120.

57 *Hansard*, 1980–1, 23 July 1981, column 498.

58 *The Times*, 10 September 1981.

59 See Lawrence Freedman, *Britain and Nuclear Weapons*, London, Macmillan, 1980; A. J. R. Groom, *British Thinking About Nuclear Weapons*, London, Pinter, 1974; Margaret Gowing, *Independence and Deterrence* (2 vols), London, Macmillan, 1974.

60 *The Times*, 29 October 1981.

61 *Hansard*, 1980–1, 27 October 1981, column 720.

62 Lunn, *op. cit.* See also an analysis by John Barry in *The Times*, 16 November 1981.

63 Letter to *The Times*, 17 October 1981.

64 *Hansard*, 1980–1, 20 May 1981, column 298.

65 *Daily Telegraph*, 9 September 1981.

66 *The Times*, 12 September 1981.

67 *Hansard*, 1980–1, 20 May 1981, column 298.

68 *The Times*, 29 October 1981.

69 *Hansard*, 1980–1, 5 November 1981, column 122.

70 *The Times*, 5 November 1981.

71 The linking of arguments against unilateral disarmament and for continued membership of the European Community may become more salient as they are a consistent platform for the Social Democratic Party. This also offers the added advantage of distinguishing the SDP clearly from the Labour Party.

Is there a Soviet military threat?

1 *Soviet Military Power*, Washington DC, US Department of Defense, September 1981.

2 Paul Cocks, 'Rethinking the Organization Weapon: The Soviet System in a Systems Age', *World Politics*, vol. XXXIII, no. 2, 1980.

3 *The Military Balance 1981–2*, London, International Institute for Strategic Studies, 1981.

4 *World Military Expenditures and Arms Trade 1970–1979*, Washington DC, US Arms Control and Disarmament Agency, 1981.

5 IISS, *op. cit.*

6 Fred Kaplan, 'Inside the Soviet Threat', *Inquiry*, 23 November, 1981.

7 Victor Suvorov, *The Liberators*, London, Hamish Hamilton, 1981.

8 Andrew Cockburn, 'Weinberger's Statistics', *New York Times*, 13, 14 November 1981.

9 'The Red Army', *World in Action*, 13 April 1981.

10 IISS, *op. cit.*, p. 123.

11 '20 Years of Decline in the Soviet Empire', *Washington Post*, 17 March 1981.

12 *Ibid.*

13 Michael Klare, 'The Feeble Giant', *Nation*, 24 October 1981.

Nato and the states of Western Europe

1   This grows directly out of the Clausewitzian view of the relationship between military force and power: 'War is a continuation of policy by other means. Karl von Clausewitz, *On War*, Harmondsworth, Penguin Books, 1968.

2   Circular error probability (CEP) refers to the radius around a target within which 50 per cent of warheads can be guaranteed to fall. By 1985 CEPs for new missiles will be down to 200–400 metres; by 1990 down to tens of metres.

3   *The Times*, 20 October 1981.

4   *The Times*, 22 October 1981.

The threat of nuclear war and the responsibilities of scientists

1   MIRV = Multiple Independently-targetable Re-entry Vehicle. A 'MIRVed' missile may carry several separate re-entry vehicles, each with its own warhead, and each aimed at a specific target. The term 're-entry vehicle' is used because the MIRVs leave the parent missile when it is outside the earth's atmosphere and re-enter the atmosphere on their way to their targets. MIRV was introduced by the USA in 1970 and by the USSR in 1977. The long-range missile M-X and Trident are discussed later in this article.

2   George B. Kistiakowsky, *A Scientist in the White House*, Boston, Harvard University Press, 1976.

3   Kosta Tsipis, *Offensive Missiles,* Report no. 5, Stockholm International Peace Research Institute, 1974.

4   Example: An improved Minuteman III (Mark 12A warhead) is aimed against a Soviet SS-18 silo hardened to 500 psi. What is the kill probability, assuming the missile reliability to be unity ($m = 1$)? This warhead has a yield $y = 0.35$ Mt and an accuracy (circular error probability) $r = 180$ metres, or 0.097 nautical miles.

Lethality $K = (0.35)^{2/3}/(0.097)^2 = 52.8$.
For a silo of hardness $H = 500$ psi, $f(H) = 0.058$, from equation (5).
From equation (1)
$$P_K = 1 - \exp\left[-\,52.8/2 \times \{500 \times 0.058\}^{2/3}\right]$$
$$= 0.94 \text{ (or 94 per cent)}$$

5 'The long-range cruise missile', SIPRI *Yearbook*, 1980, ch. 11.

6 e.g. *The Nation*, 14 April 1979. Cruise missiles are 'SALT-free' because the warhead is so small (about 15–20 inches in diameter) that it is impossible to tell whether the warhead is nuclear or not. SALT-type agreements depend critically upon mutual verification through *remote* surveillance, an impossible option with cruise missiles.

7 For a fascinating account of the gestation of Pershing II, see the article by Christopher Paine in the *Bulletin of the Atomic Scientists*. October 1980, p. 25.

8 For an assessment of progress in anti-submarine warfare, see ch. 8 of the SIPRI *Yearbook*, 1979.

9 SIPRI *Yearbook* 1981, foreword, p. XV.

10 Lord Zuckerman, 'Scientific advisers and scientific advice', *Proceedings of the American Philosophical Society*, vol. 124, November 1980, pp. 241–55.

11 Frank Barnaby's lecture, with others on related topics, has been published in *The Nuclear Arms Race Control or Catastrophe?* Barnaby and Thomas (eds), London, F. Pinter, 1982.

12 These are known as Poseidon C4 missiles. They are MIRVed, with eight warheads per missile, each of 0.1 Mt yield. The accuracy of the C4 system is said to be 500 metres, which gives each C4 missile a total lethality of 24.

13 More information about SANA may be obtained from Barbara Pearce, 11 Church Street, Woburn Sands, Milton Keynes MK17 8PG.

A Christian response to the arms race

1 *The Times*, 4 November 1981.

2 Acts ch. 23, verse 7.

3 Dr P. Rogers, Dr M. Dando and Dr P. van den Dungen *As Lambs to the Slaughter*, London, Arrow Books, 1981.

4 The *Guardian*, 28 October 1981.

5 The Rapacki Plan (named after the Polish Foreign Minister) was proposed in 1957. It was a plan to create a nuclear-free zone comprising of Poland, Czechoslovakia and East and West Germany.

6   P. Rogers *et al, op. cit*, p. 259.

7   The Alternative Defence Commission is a new group set up to investigate alternatives to Britain's present defence policy. It has been set up by the Lansbury House Trust Fund in conjunction with the School of Peace Studies at Bradford University. The commission will be asking for submissions from trade unions, political parties, peace organisations, churches and interested individuals and will draw on the expertise of peace research and strategic studies institutes and academic specialists. It is expected that the commission will produce a report in 1982.

8   Directive 59 shifted American nuclear targeting policy from cities and centres of population to military targets. The implications of this change in official US policy indicated a willingness to fight war rather than maintain a second-strike deterrence posture.

9   Robert C. Aldridge, *The Counterforce Syndrome: A Guide to US Nuclear Weapons and Strategic Doctrine*, Washington DC, Institute of Policy Studies, 1979.

10 Max Planck Institute is located in Starnberg, West Germany and is concerned with research on security questions.

11 *North-South: A Programme for Survival*, London, Pan Books, 1980.

12 Collossians, ch. 1, verse 20.

13 St Matthew, ch. 5, verse 9.

14 St John, ch. 14, verse 27.

15 The Second Epistle of Peter, ch. 3, verses 11–13.

16 *Early Christian Writings: The Apostolic Fathers*, translated by M. Staniforth, Harmondsworth, Penguin, 1968, pp. 169–85.

The media and defence

1   The *Guardian*, 27 September 1980.

2   The *Washington Post*, 24 October 1981.

3   *The Times*, 4 December 1981.

Select bibliography

This list aims to offer the reader a selection of the most recent accessible literature. Journals containing suitable articles are also listed. The categories complement the subjects covered in the debate.

Recent strategic theorising

Aldridge, R. C., *The Counterforce Syndrome*, Washington, DC, Institute for Policy Studies, 1978.

Bertram, Christopher (ed.), *Strategic Deterrence in a Changing Environment*, London, Gower Press, 1981.

Booth, Ken, *Strategy and Ethnocentricism*, London, Croom Helm, 1979.

Brodie, Bernard, *War and Politics*, London, Cassell's, 1973.

Garnett, John (ed.), *Theories of Peace and Security*, London, Macmillan, 1970.

George, A. H., and Smoke, R., *Deterrence in American Foreign Policy: Theory and Practice*, New York, Columbia University Press, 1974.

Gompert, David, C., *et al., Nuclear Weapons and World Politics*, New York, McGraw-Hill, 1977.

Holst, Johan J. (ed.), *Beyond Nuclear Deterrence: New Aims, New Arms*, London, Macdonald and Jane's, 1977.

Mandelbaum, Michael, *The Nuclear Question*, Cambridge University Press, 1979.

Mandelbaum, Michael, *The Nuclear Revolution*, Cambridge University Press, 1981.

Martin, Laurence, *Strategic Thought in the Nuclear Age*, London, Heinemann, 1979.

Morgan, Patrick, M., *Deterrence: A Conceptual Analysis*, London, Sage Publications, 1977.

Ranger, Robin, *Arms and Politics 1958–1978: Arms Control in a Changing Political Context*, Toronto, Macmillan, 1979.

Snow, Donald M., *Nuclear Strategy in a Dynamic World: American Policy in the 1980's,* University of Alabama Press, 1981.

Speed, Roger, *Strategic Deterrence in the 1980's,* Stamford, California, Hoover Institute Press, 1979.

Stockholm International Peace Research Institute, *World Armaments: The Nuclear Threat,* Stockholm, SIPRI, 1977.

Disarmament and alternative defence strategies

Beres, Louis R., *Apocalypse: Nuclear Catastrophe in World Politics,* University of Chicago Press, 1980.

Cox, John, *Overkill,* Harmondsworth, Penguin Books, 1981.

Epstein, William and Toyoda, Toshiyuki, *A New Design for Nuclear Disarmament,* Nottingham, Spokesman Books, 1977.

Geeraerts, G. (ed.), *Possibilities of Civilian Defence in Western Europe,* Amsterdam, Swets and Zeitlinger, 1977.

Goodwin, P. *Nuclear War: The Facts on Our Survival,* London, Ash and Grant, 1981.

Griffiths, F., and Polanyi, J. C., *The Dangers of Nuclear War,* University of Toronto Press, 1980.

Myrdal, Alva, *The Game of Disarmament,* Nottingham, Spokesman Books, 1977.

Neild, Robert, *How to Make Your Mind Up About The Bomb,* London, Andre Deutsch, 1981.

Roberts, Adam, *Nations in Arms: The Theory and Practice of Territorial Defence,* London, Chatto & Windus, 1976.

Rogers, Paul, Dando, Malcolm, and van den Dunden, Peter, *As Lambs To The Slaughter,* London, Arrow Books, 1981.

Russell, Bertrand, *Common Sense and Nuclear Warfare,* London, George Allen & Unwin, 1959.

Thompson, E. P., and Smith, D., *Protest and Survive,* Harmondsworth, Penguin Books, 1980.

European defence

Baylis, John (ed.), *British Defence Policy in a Changing World,* London, Croom Helm, 1977.

Van Cleave, W. R., and Cohen, S. T. *Tactical Nuclear Weapons: An Examination of the Issues,* London, Macdonald & Jane, 1978.

Cook, Robin and Smith, Dan, *What Future in NATO?* London, Fabian Society, 1978.

Czempiel, Ernst-Otto and Rustow, D. A., *The Euro-American System: Economic and Political Relations between North America and Western Europe*, Boulder, Colorado, Westview Press, 1976.

Freedman, Lawrence, *Britain and Nuclear Weapons*, London, Macmillan, 1980.

Groom, A. J. R., *British Thinking About Nuclear Weapons*, London, F. Pinter, 1974.

Hazel, D. and Williams, P., *The British Defence Effort: Foundations and Alternatives*, University of Aberdeen, 1978.

Hill-Norton, Peter, *No Soft Options: The Politico-Military Realities of NATO*, London, C. Hurst, 1979.

Kaldor, Mary, *The Disintegrating West*, London, Allen Lane, 1978.

Smart, Ian, *The Future of the British Nuclear Deterrent: Technical, Economic and Strategic Issues*, London, Royal Institute for International Affairs, 1977.

Smith, Dan, *The Defence of the Realm in the 1980s*, London, Croom Helm, 1980.

Treverton, Gregory, *Nuclear Weapons in Europe* (Adelphi Paper 168), London, International Institute for Strategic Studies, 1981.

The Soviet threat

Bahro, Rudolph, *The Alternative in Eastern Europe*, London, New Left Books, 1978.

Baylis, J and Segal, G. (eds), *Soviet Strategy*, London, Croom Helm, 1981.

Blechman, B. M., *et al.*, *The Soviet Military Build Up and United States Defence Spending*, Washington DC, Brookings Institution, 1977.

Douglass, Joseph D. and Hoeber, A. M., *Soviet Strategy for Nuclear War*, Stanford, Hoover Institute Press, 1979.

Douglass, Joseph D., *Soviet Military Strategy in Europe*, Oxford, Pergamon Press, 1980.

Haselkorn, Avigdor, *The Evolution of Soviet Security Strategy, 1965–1975*, New York, Crane Russak, 1978.

Kirk, G. and Wessell, N., *The Soviet Threat: Myths and Realities*, New York, Praeger, 1978.

Kaplan, F., *Dubious Spectre: A Sceptical Look at the Soviet Nuclear Threat*, Washington DC, Institute for Policy Studies, 1980.

Whetten, Laurence, *The Future of Soviet Military Power*, New York, Crane Russak, 1976.

Scientific aspects

Burt, Richard, *New Weapons Technologies: Debate and Directions*, (Adelphi Paper 126), London, International Institute for Strategic Studies, 1976.

Carlton, David and Schaerf, Carlo, *Arms Control and Technological Innovation*, London, Croom Helm, 1977.

Glasstone, S. and Dolan, P. J., *The Effects of Nuclear Weapons*, Tunbridge Wells, Castle House, 1980.

Melman, S., *The Permanent War Economy,* New York, Simon & Schuster, 1975.

Pentz, Michael, *Towards the Final Abyss?*, London, J. D. Bernal Peace Library, 1980.

Russett, Bruce M., and Blair, Bruce G., *Progress in Arms Control?* (Readings from *Scientific American*), San Francisco, Freeman, 1979.

Ethical aspects

Best, G., *Humanity in Warfare*, London, Weidenfeld & Nicolson, 1981.

Ford, Harold P. and Francis Winters (eds.), *Ethics and Nuclear Strategy*, New York, Orbis Books, 1977.

Green, Philip, *Deadly Logic: The Theory of Nuclear Deterrence*, Ohio State University Press, 1966.

Kaplan, Morton (ed.), *Strategic Thinking and its Moral Implications*, University of Chicago Press, 1973.

Rachels, J. (ed.), *Moral Problems: A Collection of Philosophical Essays*, New York, Harper & Row, 1975.

Ramsey, Paul, *The Just War: Force and Political Responsibility*, New York, Scribners, 1968.

Paskins, Barrie and Dockrill, Michael, *The Ethics of War*, London, Duckworth, 1979.

Stein, Walter (ed.), *Nuclear Weapons: A Catholic Response*, London, Merlin Press, 1965.

Stein, W., *Nuclear Weapons and Christian Conscience*, London, Merlin Press, 1981.

Walzer, Michael, *Just and Unjust Wars,* Harmondsworth, Penguin Books, 1977.

CND Christian Pamphlet, 'Blessed Are The Peacemakers', 1981.

Democracy and disarmament

Bunyard, Peter, *Nuclear Britain*, London, New English Library, 1981.

Ryle, M. H., *The Politics of Nuclear Disarmament*, Pluto Press, London 1981.

Smith, Dan (ed.), *Alternative World for Military Industries*, London, Richardson Institute, 1977.

Kaldor, M., Smith, D., and Vines, S. (eds), *Democratic Socialism and the Cost of Defence*, London, Croom Helm, 1979.

Journals and reference works

Adelphi Papers	a series of occasional papers from the International Institute for Strategic Studies covering many detailed aspects of strategy.
Armament and Disarmament Information Unit Report	from University of Sussex, provides information on recent developments, and detailed sources.
Bulletin of the Atomic Scientists	a useful factual source providing both technical and social material on the many aspects of nuclear power.
E.N.D. Bulletin	newsletter of the European Nuclear Disarmament campaign, offering an international perspective.
Foreign Affairs	published in the United States, and covering many issues concerned with US foreign and defence policy.
International Affairs	published by the Royal Institute of International Affairs and includes many articles on the defence policies of various countries.
The Journal of Strategic Studies	dealing with theoretical and practical issues.
The Military Balance	published by the International Institute for Strategic Studies as an annual listing of the military hardware of all countries.
New Scientist	publishes many articles on the technical aspects of the arms race, and nuclear power in general.

Orbis	published in the US and including many articles on aspects of strategic thought.
Peace News	orientated towards the pacifist perspective and publishes reports on the disarmament campaigns.
Royal United States Institute Journal	deals mainly with detailed military and technical issues of armaments and strategy.
Sanity	the newspaper of the Campaign for Nuclear Disarmament.
Scientific American	includes many articles on technical aspects of nuclear weapons.
Stockholm International Peace Research Institute	publishes many books and works of reference, in particular the annual SIPRI *Armaments and Disarmament Yearbook.*
Strategic Survey	published annually by the International Institute for Strategic Studies as an overview of major conflicts and tensions.
Survival	published bi-monthly by the International Institute for Strategic Studies, dealing with strategic problems in articles and reference material.
World Politics	published in the United States, including frequent articles on the theories of strategy and conflict.
World Today	published by the Royal Institute of International Affairs and includes many articles commenting on contemporary strategic and European issues.

Index